HOME·BREWED

BEER & CIDER

About the Author

Ben Turner has been brewing his own beers since 1952, when it was still necessary to have a licence to brew at home. He made his first cider two years later from cider apples given to him during a visit to Somerset and continues to make it whenever apples are plentiful.

He started writing and lecturing about home brewing in 1958 and has since had more than thirty books published on the subject. Five of these have also been published in Canada and another in Australia and New Zealand.

In 1959, Ben Turner founded the Harrow Guild of Winemakers and two years later was a co-founder of the National Association of Amateur Winemakers. In 1963, he was a co-founder and first Honorary Secretary of the Amateur Winemakers' National Guild of Judges and, from 1971 to 1973, President of the re-named National Association of Wine and Beermakers.

In 1974, Ben Turner became a full-time author and lecturer on home brewing and has since devised television programmes both for the BBC and ITV and broadcasts frequently on radio. He is, in addition, a senior lecturer in the Adult Education Service both of Harrow and Hillingdon.

Acknowledgements

The Author wishes to acknowledge the ready and friendly assistance accorded to him by the Taunton Cider Company, and especially by Mr Bradstock.

The Author and Publisher are grateful to the following for permission to include copyright material:
The Brewers Society for providing photographs to be used as artist's references.
The Mansell Collection, for the picture on p.14, and Whitbread and Company Limited, for the picture on p.12.

Design by Etchell and Ridyard
Artwork by A. L. Gardiner
Cover photography by John Chilton

Published by EP Publishing Limited, East Ardsley, Wakefield, Yorkshire WF3 2JN, England
This edition published 1981 by Book Club Associates.
By arrangement with EP Publishing Limited.

Printed by Chorley & Pickersgill Ltd Leeds

HOME·BREWED
BEER & CIDER

BY
BEN TURNER

ep
E P Publishing Limited

Book Club
Associates
London

Background to Brewing 6

A Brewer's Glossary 16

Different Beer Styles 23

Basic Processes of Brewing 28

Equipment for Home Brewing 32
Kits 32
Malt Extract and Hops Method 33
The Grain Mash Method 35

Ingredients for Home Brewing 37
Water 37
Malt 39
Adjuncts 39
Hops 41
Sugar 42
Yeast 42

Brewing Beers at Home 44
Hygiene 44

From Kits 45
From Malt Extract and Hops 48
Grain Mash Beers 50
Serving Beer 51

Recipes for Beers 53
Kits 53
Malt Extract and Hops 54
 Basic Bitter 54
 Variations 57

Grain Mash Beers 58
 Bitter Beer 59
 Brown Ale 61
 Dry Stout 61
 Milk Stout 61
 Barley Wine 62
 Lager 62

Unusual Beers 63
 Cock Ale 63

Contents

Honey Beer   64
Treacle Ale   64
Fruit Ales   64
Ginger Beer   65

Cider Making — Past and Present   66

Basic Principles of Cider Making   71

Equipment for Cider Making   75

Cider Making at Home   78
Preparation   79
Washing   79
Crushing   80
Pressing   80
Improving the Juice   81
Checking for Sugar   81
Prepare the Yeast   82

Fermentation   83
Stuck Ferment   83
Racking   84
Fining   85
Filtering   85
Bottling   86
Blending   86
Sparkling Cider   87
Vintage Cider   87
Cooking with Cider   87
Faults and Remedies   88

Cider Recipes   90
Everyday Cider   90
Country Cider   91
Sweet Cider   92
Scrumpy   92
Cider Vinegar   94

Tables   95

Background to Brewing

There is evidence to support the belief that beer has been brewed for the last 5000 years. Impressions of the barleycorn — the basic ingredient of beer — have been found in pieces of pottery that have been dated around 3000 BC. Traces of other cultivated cereals have also been found in pottery that archaeologists are sure were used between the Neolithic and Viking periods.

It is believed that cultivated barley was first grown in Egypt and that knowledge of the process of brewing an alcoholic drink from it came to England with the Phoenicians who were trading in the tin then being mined in Cornwall. The slaves who built the Pyramids were given a kind of ale, although the Pharaohs and Nobles drank wine.

Early brewing in England

There is no certain evidence of when ale was first brewed in England. There is a good deal of circumstantial evidence, however, to indicate that an ale was brewed before the Romans came in 55 BC. A coin has been found from the first century BC, on one side of which is depicted an ear of cultivated barley.

Julius Caesar noted that the south-eastern part of England was well populated and that corn was widely grown. We know from Roman writings that 'cerevisia', the Latin name for ale, was made in Europe, and there is no reason why it should not also have been made in England. There are a number of references to alcoholic drinks in the writings of Biblical times, so we know that the concept of fermentation was appreciated.

With the growth of Christianity, more certain evidence became available. Gildas, a monk living in the fifth century AD, admonished his brother monks thus, 'If any monk through drinking too freely gets thick of speech so that he cannot join the psalmody, he is to be deprived of his supper.' In the sixth century, St David added his proscription on drunkenness and awarded penalties of penance on those monks who were caught. In the seventh century, Theodore, the seventh Archbishop of Canterbury (668-93), prescribed penance for laymen found guilty of drunkenness. King Hlother and King Eadric of Kent (673-85) also decreed punishments for drunkenness, involving the taking-away of a man's 'stoup' or mug of ale. If drunkenness was so rife, much ale must have been brewed!

There is evidence that ale was brewed in Ireland before the arrival of St Patrick in 432. Welsh ale, too, is sometimes mentioned in the early records.

The Vikings were great drinkers of ale and their invasion of England in 793 no doubt stimulated brewing here. Indeed, it is thought that our word ale comes from the Saxon *elau* (Danish *öl*). The word beer is thought to have Teutonic origins and the Anglo-Saxons used both words to mean the same beverage. Later the meanings changed and beer became the description of an ale flavoured with hops.

By the end of the ninth century, ale-houses existed not only in towns and villages, but also along the old Roman roads. King Edgar (959-75) thought that the cause of drunkenness among so many of his people was this great number of ale-houses, so he tried to close many of them and limit them to one per village. He also decreed that there should be one standard of measurement and one standard of weight, but he did not have the means to enforce his decrees and they were largely ignored. There was another attempt to deal with the problem of measurement in the Magna Carta, in 1215. This met with a greater measure of success, probably because by this time royal authority extended more thoroughly over the country and more officials existed to enforce the law.

The Norman Conquest

Following the Norman Conquest in 1066, there is frequent mention in documents of the annual payment of 'ales' to the lord of the manor. By this time, ale was brewed in almost every home — as bread was also baked. Both strong and weak ales were brewed. Because of the lack of sanitation, it was often safer to drink a weak ale than to drink water, since the ale had to be boiled in the process of brewing. It was customary to give it to children of all ages.

An interesting record exists of a consignment of ale sent to the French Court in 1158. Because of the ready availability of wine, the French had not become brewers and they marvelled at the English ale. It was described as 'most wholesome, clear of all dregs, equalling wine in colour and surpassing it in flavour'.

Perhaps this noble praise gave ideas to Henry II, for not many years later, in 1188, he levied the first national tax on ale. The money went towards the war against Saladin and was known as the Saladin Tithe. Once started, taxation of fermented beverages has never stopped.

That brewing ale was a major cottage industry is clear from a decree made in 1189. It was concerned with precautions against the risk of fire. Ale-wives were 'forbidden to brew by night with straw or stubble, but only with wood'. This is one of the earliest recognitions of women as the predominant brewers and retailers of ale.

The price and quality of the ale they brewed varied substantially. In 1267, Henry III introduced the 'Assize of Bread and Ale' which controlled the ale-wives' prices for the next 300 years. In 1276 a London Assize court determined that the price of one gallon of particular ale must not exceed three farthings and another must not exceed one penny. In 1283, an Assize in Bristol also refers to two types of ale.

Ale-conners

Control was now exercised on the quantity and price, but the control of quality was another matter. There were no objective ways of comparing an ale with a standard and so subjective methods had to be employed. Ale-conners were appointed in each area to taste the ales before they were sold. The conner had the authority to downgrade an ale in price if, in his opinion, it was not of fair value for the price charged. Conners often wore leather breeches and some would pour ale on a seat and then sit in it for half an hour. If, when the conner rose, the seat stuck to his breeches, the ale was deemed not to have been properly fermented and was condemned. If the conner could leave his seat without difficulty, the ale was declared good. After each new brew, an ale-wife was obliged to draw the attention of the ale-conner by the erection outside her house of a branch of a tree known as an ale-stake.

A further record from this fascinating period in the development of brewing concerns the tax returns of one parti-

cular town in 1327. Of the 252 tradespeople who paid tax, 84 were brewers, all of whom were women!

Thirteen years later in 1340, a brewery was installed at Queen's College, Oxford. Ale was brewed there for the staff and scholars for the next six hundred years and was only discontinued after the last war.

Unflavoured and hopped ales

Up to the end of the fourteenth century, ale was frequently sold unflavoured with herbs or hops. Individual ale-wives sometimes used nettles, yarrow, rowan or fruits such as blackberries or elderberries, or even a flayed cockerel. At the beginning of the fifteenth century, however, some hopped ale was imported into Winchelsea from Flanders. This started a controversy that lasted 100 years. The flavour of this beer, as it was called, was quite enjoyed by some and the demand grew. Hops were not grown in England at that time and had to be imported from Holland. Nevertheless, some brewers started to flavour their ale with hops in spite of the animosity of the 'real ale' brewers. The Mystery of Ale Brewers was controlled as to the price they could charge for defined quantities and also to the quality. Furthermore, they were subject to local and national taxations. Beer brewers, on the other hand, were not so controlled, but competition was coming from disreputable brewers of poor beer. Official recognition of beer was becoming important to the new brewers. In 1464 they petitioned the Mayor and Aldermen of the City of London to form their own Mystery. Although this was granted, prejudice against beer continued from the ale brigade. In 1471 at Norwich, the local use of hops and 'gawle' was forbidden.

By 1482, beer brewers were officially recognised for tax purposes and were charged a duty of twenty shillings on each barrel of thirty-six gallons of beer. Ale brewers were exempt from this particular duty and the bitterness between the two factions continued. In 1484, the ale brewers of London, concerned at the increasing popularity of beer, petitioned 'that hoppes, herbs and the like, be not used in ale, only liquor, malt and yeste'. The petition was granted and a fine of six shillings and eight pence was imposed on every barrel of ale not brewed according to these regulations. Nine years later in 1493, the beer brewers were fully accepted and within fifty years, hops were used for flavouring both ale and beer. Even so, pockets of resistance continued and local laws were made in 1512 in

Shrewsbury, forbidding the use of that 'wicked and pernicious weed, hops'. Another was made in Coventry in 1513, where it was decreed that 'no bruer in this cittie brue any ale with hoppes'.

In 1524, Flemish immigrants settled in Kent, planted hops and began an activity that continues until this day.

Ale played a significant part in all social activities. The monks were great brewers, not only for their own use, but also for those who availed themselves of the hospitality of the monasteries, so generously given. Money was raised for the repair of churches and bridges by selling ale. Taxes were paid with ale. Drinking contests were held. Beer became the national beverage.

Coopers flourished and, in 1409, formed a Mystery to maintain standards of craftmanship. Every cooper had his own sign and a branding iron to mark his cask. A record of these signs was kept at the Guildhall, so that the maker of any cask could be traced.

Innholders, too, formed the Mystery of Hostelers and asked that their members be enfranchised in the Craft of Hostelers. In 1473, they changed their name to Innholders. The industry was flourishing in all its aspects and all those who traded in the industry in the City of London had to pay a tax to the Lord Mayor. It was often referred to as 'ale silver'.

The first licensing laws

In 1495, the first licensing laws were passed, but a more important Act of 1552 gave Justices of the Peace the power not only to license ale-houses, but also to supress them when deemed necessary. Ale-houses sold only ale and beer, usually brewed on the premises. Taverns sold ale, beer and wine. Inns not only sold ale, beer and wine, but also provided refreshment and accommodation for travellers, their servants and their horses.

Hitherto taken for granted, the making of malt now received the attention of the law. An act was passed in 1548 for the proper making of malt. The purpose was to prevent under-dried and poorly made malt from being supplied to the brewers. Experience showed that malt deteriorated rapidly if it was not properly made, and consequently the resulting beer was inferior.

With the dissolution of the monasteries at the time of the Reformation, the brewing of ale and beer steadily moved away from the ale-houses, taverns and inns. The displaced

An eighteenth century
brewery

12

monk-brewers, usually very highly skilled, were often employed by entrepreneur brewers who sold their excellent beverages to the less skilled retailers. Gradually these breweries increased in size and it is recorded that in 1591, some 26400 barrels of beer were exported from London.

Duty imposed on beer

The Stuart period is best remembered in the brewing industry for the establishment of Customs and Excise duties. At one time, in a total annual revenue of £1,200,000 as much as £500,000 came from ale and beer. In 1653, even home brewers were taxed. No doubt this tax was difficult to collect and the law was dropped for a time.

The growth of modern breweries

By the eighteenth century, some of the big names in brewing today became established. They included Bass, Courage, Coombe, Charrington Simmonds, Watney, Whitbread and Worthington. The publican brewers and the domestic brewers declined in number, although many lingered on in isolated places. The saccharimeter, for measuring the quantity of sugar in a wort, and the thermometer, for measuring its temperature, were invented. The beginnings of scientific control were introduced.

At this time, in the early 1700s, the public had the choice of three different beers — brown, old and pale ale. Some people drank these half and half or a third from each cask. About 1720, the London brewers produced a beer consisting of a blend of these three styles and called it Entire. The beer became popular with manual workers, especially the London porters, and the name of the beer was changed to Porter. It was

13

brewed in Sheffield in 1744 and in Glasgow in 1775. Eventually this popular, soft-water beer was brewed in Ireland, where it continued to be popular long after its brewing was discontinued everywhere else.

Humulus lupulus (hops)

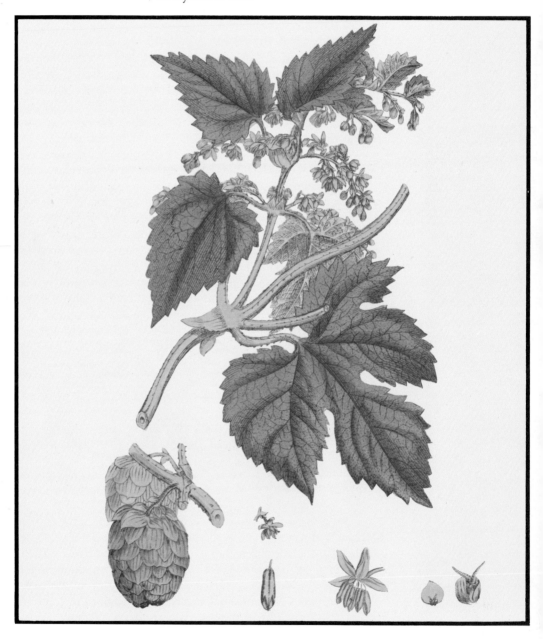

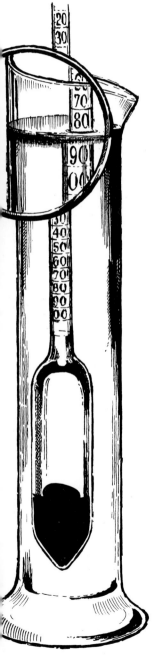

Duty is levied on original gravity

London had become famous for its soft-water beers and Burton-on-Trent for its tangy, crisp, bitter beers. Indeed, Burton beer was much exported to the Baltic area as well as other markets in Europe, Africa, America and the West Indies. Export of ale to India was largely in the hands of a London brewer named Hodgson. He developed the strong, well-hopped beer that has become known as India Pale Ale and is still known as I.P.A. or Export ale.

During the nineteenth century, there were developments in the production of better hops — notably East Kent Goldings and West Kent Fuggles. The addition of sugar was legally permitted in order to increase alcohol content, the taxes on malt and hops were repealed, and a new tax on the original gravity of the wort was introduced. This is still the basis of Excise duty and has caused a general lowering of the strength and quality of beer ever since. This tax of 1880 also applied to the domestic brewer and remained in force for more than eighty years until 1963. In that year the Chancellor of the Exchequer removed the tax on home brewers since it had become uneconomical to collect it. The brewing of good beers at home started all over again.

In the commercial world, other controls were introduced. These included the time at which public houses may open and close, and the number of hours that they must remain open. Service to children and young persons was forbidden, as were the playing of music, dancing, shows and so on unless especially licensed.

In recent years, the amalgamation of breweries with the consequent increase in overheads, taken in conjunction with the many restrictions and yet another tax, VAT, has contributed to the decline in quality and the increase in the prices of pub beers. The Campaign for Real Ale is having some effect in halting the decline in quality, but several million British families have now reverted to brewing at least some of the beer they drink.

Home brewing
Modern equipment and technology and the ready availability of fine ingredients have brought the brewing of excellent beer at home within the capabilities of everyone. In the chapters that follow, the equipment, ingredients and technology are described in a manner for all to understand and follow.

A Brewer's Glossary

Brewers have a specialist vocabulary just like those in other crafts. The word liquor, for example, means not the finished beer as might be expected, but only the water from which the beer is made. The following list of words and their meaning will be found helpful in understanding the different equipment, ingredients and processes of brewing. It is by no means exhaustive, since it contains only the more common words that are met. Highly technical words have been omitted because they are beyond the scope of this book.

Acetic acid. The sharp-smelling, sharp-tasting acid found in vinegar. It is caused by mycoderma aceti and other micro-organisms that reduce beer to vinegar in the presence of air. Hence the reason for keeping wort and beer well covered and the vessels full, thus excluding air. Technically, it is the alcohol in the beer that is reduced to vinegar.

Acrospire. The tiny shoot that is produced from a grain of barley during the malting process.

16

Adjuncts. Starch containing substances added to malt grains prior to mashing, in order to increase the original gravity of the wort and to enhance the texture and flavour.

Alcohol. The spirit that gives beer its 'satisfaction'. It is one of the products of fermentation. It is more correctly described as ethyl alcohol since this is 90 per cent of its content. Other alcohols present in minute quantities include amyl, butyl, propyl, methyl, glycerol, etc.

Aldehyde. The initial product of the oxidation of alcohol and a contributor to the good smell of beer.

Ale. Formerly an unhopped beer. Now synonymous with beer.

Aroma. The quality of fragrance when applied to dried hops or a finished beer.

Attenuation. The reduction of the original gravity of beer during the process of fermentation.

Barley. The cereal grain most commonly used for malting and thence brewing into beer. Wheat and maize are sometimes used, but not oats or rye.

Barrel. A wooden, stainless steel or plastic container capable of holding 36 Imperial gallons of beer. The word is also used as a unit of measure.

Beer. An ale flavoured with hops. When other flavourings are used, the name of the flavouring is used to describe the beer, e.g. ginger beer.

Bramling. The name of a hop variety.

Brewers' gold. The name of a hop variety.

Brewers' yeast. The species saccharomyces cerevisiae. Saccharomyces means sugar fungi, cerevisiae comes from the Latin word meaning beer. The top fermenting variety is mainly used in Britain. It is globular in shape, ferments rapidly and forms both part of the frothy head that develops on wort during fermentation and the putty-coloured paste left in the bottom of the bin after racking. It is a single-celled plant invisible to the naked eye.

17

Bullion. The name of a hop variety.

Burton. The name of the most famous brewing town in England. The water from its wells is particularly hard and imparts a crisp, tangy taste to beer. The name Burton is now used to describe that style of bitter beer whether brewed in Burton or not.

Calcium sulphate. The mineral salt that imparts the hard quality to water. It is often added, together with magnesium sulphate, to soft water to make it hard.

Caramel. The name used for burnt sugar. Nowadays, it is usually made by heating glucose with ammonium salts. It is sometimes added to a wort to improve the colour of a beer, but its bitter flavour has to be taken into account.

Carbon dioxide. The gas given off during the fermentation of sugar into alcohol by yeast. It is also the sparkle and life in a mature beer.

Cask. A small container for beer, usually a pin [4½ gallons (20.5 litres)] or a firkin [9 gallons (41 litres)] or even a kilderkin [18 gallons (82 litres)]. For home brewers, most casks are made from plastic materials and hold some 5½ gallons (25 litres), but some smaller ones have recently been marketed as well.

Condition. The quantity of carbon dioxide contained in a finished beer, hence 'out of condition' for a flat beer, i.e. one that is lifeless and without carbon dioxide. It also refers to the presence in hops of the golden-yellow dust, lupulin, that contains the resins that provide the preservative so necessary to keep a beer tasty.

Cytase. An enzyme which exists in barley grains and which dissolves the cellulose covering of the starch during malting.

Dextrin. Substances released during the mashing of the grains. Some dextrins are unfermentable and give body and sweetness to beer.

Diastase. Really two different enzymes known as alpha amylase and beta amylase. They cause the starch to break down into dextrin and maltose during the mashing process.

18

Draught. The term used to describe a beer that is served from a cask rather than a bottle.

Dry hopping. The addition of a small amount of dry hops to a fermenting wort to improve the flavour of the beer.

End point. The stage in the mashing process when the diastase has converted all the starch in the grains into dextrin and maltose. It is usually reached between two and four hours after mashing has started.

Fermentation. The process in which the maltose is converted first into glucose and then, through a complicated chain of reactions, into alcohol and carbon dioxide.

Finings. Substances used for removing the haze of suspended particles from a finished beer.

Flakes. An abbreviation for flaked rice, flaked maize and flaked barley. These are all adjuncts used in the preparation of certain beers to improve their quality.

Flocculence. The cloudy swirl of yeast made when moving a container of unracked beer. It is caused by a fault in the yeast and has to be removed by fining and possibly by filtering, too.

Fructose. One of the two monosaccharide components of sucrose, household sugar. It is sometimes called levulose.

Fuggles. The name of a hop variety commonly used for flavouring brown ales and stouts. Now being replaced by Wye Northdown.

Fusel oil. One of the higher alcohols formed during fermentation and caused by the breakdown of the amino acids. The main constituent is amyl alcohol. A trace adds to the bouquet and flavour. In excess it has an adverse effect on both.

Gallon. A unit of measure equal to eight Imperial pints. Its metric equivalent is 4.546 litres. Most beer is brewed in gallons or pints.

Gelatin. A fining agent often used to clear hazy beers.

Glucose. The other of the two monosaccharide components of sucrose. See also Fructose. It is sometimes called dextrose. It is often sold to home brewers in the form of 'chips' and is used in preference to household sugar.

Goldings. A hop variety commonly used for bitter beers, but being replaced by Wye Challenger.

Grist. The terms used for the malt grains or mixture of grains before crushing. Hence, 'all grist for the mill'. Also called 'goods'.

Grits. Untreated grain such as maize or rice before adding to the grist.

Hallertau. A variety of hop originating from Bavaria and used for flavouring lager.

Hardening salts. A mixture of calcium and magnesium sulphates with traces of other minerals, used to harden water for the brewing, anywhere, of Burton-type beers.

Head. The creamy foam on the top of a glass of beer. It indicates that the beer is in good condition.

Hop. The female flower of the hop plant, humulus lupulus, used for flavouring and preserving beer.

Hop oil. The concentrated essence of hops, sometimes added to a fermenting wort instead of dry hops to improve the flavour. It should not be used as a substitute for hops in the preparation of the wort.

Hop pellets. Ground-up hop flowers compressed into small tablets. They can be more easily stored in vapour-proof containers. Ideal for the home brewer.

Hopping rate. The quantity of hops used per gallon or barrel.

Hydrometer. An instrument used by brewers to measure the specific or original gravity of the wort prior to fermentation. This indicates the potential alcohol content of the finished beer. If the figure is too low, a little more malt or glucose may be

added. If it is too high, the wort may be diluted with water or a thinner beer.

Invert sugar. The name given to a mixture of glucose and fructose that is ready for fermentation. It is sometimes used in preference to household sugar to ensure a speedy fermentation when added to a wort.

Isinglass. A fining agent sometimes used to clear a hazy beer.

Lactose. A sugar that cannot be fermented by brewers' yeast. It is the sugar found in milk and is sometimes used to sweeten stouts and brown ales.

Lees. The deposit of dead yeast, hop particles and other solids that settle on the bottom of a vessel during and immediately after the fermentation of a wort into beer.

Liquor. The term used for water in the brewing of beer.

Lupulin. The resin glands produced at the bases of the bracts of each hop cone. They contain the essential brewing ingredients.

Malt. Barley grains that have been so treated by warmth and moisture that the starch has become available for conversion into fermentable sugars.

Maltose. The fermentable sugar produced from malted grains by the diastase enzymes during mashing.

Mash. The mixture of malt grains, adjuncts and hot water before and during the extraction of the maltose and dextrins.

Malt extract. A toffee-like, thick syrup prepared from a malt wort by evaporation in a vacuum. It contains about 80 per cent solids.

Malt flour. A malt extract that has been dried and spun into a powder.

Mashing. The infusion of the mash for a period of time at a specific temperature to convert the starch into maltose and dextrin.

Mashing bin. A container used for mashing.

Nutrient. Nitrogenous salts and vitamin B1 added to a wort to boost the fermenting action of the yeast.

Original gravity. The specific gravity of a wort prior to fermentation.

Pint. A unit of Imperial measure equivalent to 20fl oz (560ml).

Pitch. The action of adding an active yeast to a wort.

Priming. The addition of a small amount of fermentable sugar to a fully fermented beer at the time of bottling or casking. It causes a secondary fermentation under pressure that will give condition and liveliness to the beer.

Rack. To remove a clear or clearing beer from its lees. It is usually performed with the aid of a siphon.

Rousing. The stirring or mixing up of a liquid — the wort.

Saaz. A variety of hop originating from Bohemia and used for lager.

Sparging. The washing of the grains after mashing to extract the last traces of fermentable sugar and other soluble ingredients.

Specific gravity. The weight of a liquid compared with the weight of the same volume of water at a temperature of 59°F (15°C).

Styrian. A variety of hop originating from Slovenia and used in brewing Continental-type beers.

Sulphite. An abbreviation for sodium or potassium metabisulphite. When dissolved in water, sulphur dioxide is released. A sulphite solution is used for sterilising equipment and containers before use.

Wort. The name given to a solution of malt. It may have been prepared by mashing grains or by dissolving malt extract or malt flour in warm water.

Hop flowers

Different
Beer Styles

Britain ranks only tenth in the international beer drinkers' league, reputedly drinking 206 pints (120 litres) per head of population per year. West Germany is first, drinking 260 pints (150 litres), closely followed by Belgium, Czechoslovakia and Australia. Then comes New Zealand, Luxembourg, Denmark, Ireland and East Germany. But in none of these countries have the consumers such a wide range of beers available to them as in Britain. British beers taste different from those brewed in other countries, but once their qualities have been appreciated they are greatly enjoyed.

The range of beers available in most British pubs may well include all or most of the following, often with variations and usually with some Continental beers as well.

Keg Beers

These are usually pale ales and bitter beers that have been fermented out and distributed by the brewer without 'condition'. A quantity of carbon dioxide is injected into the beer by the bar machine when it is dispensed into the glass. Such beers are

Country	Litres per head of population per year
West Germany	150
Belgium	143
Czechoslovakia	142
Australia	142
New Zealand	133
Luxembourg	129
Denmark	128
Ireland	126
Great Britain	120*
East Germany	118
Austria	104
Canada	86
U.S.A.	82

*about 211 pints

usually the weakest and least expensive in the range. They can be easily produced in the home but usually something better is preferred.

Mild ales

These are made with an assortment of variations, but they are nearly always draught beers. They are only lightly hopped, hence the 'mild', and are low in alcohol — around 3 per cent. The colour varies with the malt — between golden and brown. Sometimes an all-pale malt is used, more often a small quantity of coloured malt is included. These ales are lightly conditioned and often have a slightly sweet taste. Because of its simplicity, this beer is always called ale and is nearest to some of the medieval beers.

Bitter beers

The most popular of the draught beers. They are usually copper coloured, i.e. a bright golden-brown, and heavily hopped, mainly with East Kent Goldings. They are malty flavoured and full bodied to balance the bitterness, but have a somewhat dry taste. They are stronger than a mild ale — around 4 per cent alcohol and again, only lightly conditioned. Both mild and bitter

beers are often pulled with a good head but this often dies quickly. Some people find the bitterness too much and dilute the beer with an equal quantity of mild ale. Bitter beers vary substantially from brewer to brewer, depending on the quantity of malt and the kind of hops used. Fine, draught bitter beers can be brewed in the home to suit your own taste.

Burton Ales

These vary in colour, flavour, strength and body, but are nearly always bottled. The different types include pale luncheon ales, bitter beers, I.P.A. or Export ales. A good Burton-Style ale has a strong flavour of tangy hops, often a blend of Goldings with Bullion, Northern brewer or Bramling. It should be full-bodied, malty and strong — around 5 per cent alcohol. It should also be well conditioned with a good and lively bead of bubbles that last throughout the time it takes to drink. The carbon dioxide imparts a freshness to the beer and contributes to its thirst-quenching qualities. Bottled light ales are usually less strong; the 'light' referring to the amount of alcohol in the beer. Export ales are usually the strongest to help the beer withstand the journey. These beers can all be made in the home to suit your own palate. If well conditioned and securely sealed, they will mature and keep for a year and longer.

Brown Ales

These, too, are normally bottled beers. They are brewed with a quantity of chocolate-coloured malt to impart both colour and flavour. They are usually lightly hopped with a Fuggles variety and are commonly low in alcohol — around 3.5 per cent. They are mashed at a temperature that extracts more insoluble dextrin from the grains, thus adding to the body and sweetness of the beer. They are a darker, bottled version of a mild ale.

Old Strong Ales

These are heavy, strong-flavoured beers, more often used for blending or cooking than for drinking by the pint. Darker than other beers except brown ales, they are produced either as draught old ale or bottled strong ale. Their alcohol content can be as high as 6 per cent and they must be hopped to match. Their popularity is declining, even among home brewers.

Black Beers and Stouts

These can be either sweet or dry. The sweet version often contains an addition of lactose that also imparts a slightly milky flavour. It is often of a low alcohol content — around 3 per cent — and brewed with some barley, roasted until it is black and caramelised but not carbonised. This adds flavour and colour but not alcohol. Fuggle hops are widely used for this sweet stout. The dry version is stronger, around 4 per cent alcohol, and more bitter than the sweet version. Both are well conditioned and hold their heads well. Both versions can be made at home and benefit from longer maturation.

A much stronger version, around 10 per cent alcohol, is sometimes made by enthusiasts and called Russian stout. This is a first cousin of barley wine, although technically it is a stout because of the malt used.

Barley Wine

This is an extremely strong, dark brown beer with an alcohol content of between 10 and 11 per cent. Fermentation takes three weeks instead of five days, and after fining and priming, maturation takes about one year. Barley wine is marketed in small bottles called 'nips', since even half a pint would be more than most people could drink. Apart from the patience factor,

Twelfth century inn
in Somerset

this beer presents no problems to the home brewer, especially
if that person is also a winemaker.

Lagers

These are pale, golden-coloured beers, brewed from Continental barley and flavoured with Hallertau or Saaz hops. They are fermented very slowly at a low temperature with saccharomyces carlsbergensis, a bottom fermenting yeast. Fermentation can take as long as three weeks. Lagers have an alcohol content around 4.5 per cent, are well hopped, of medium body and quite dry on the palate. They need to be well conditioned and long matured. A good lager is a superb drink, but many British lagers are poorly made and little better than a pale ale. A good lager is not so easy to make as many other beers, but the experienced home brewer can often do remarkably well.

General

These are the main beer styles but they are often varied by brewers to suit their own interpretation of the style. It follows that in different pubs one can find wide differences in the same general style. The same is true of home brewers. The colour, aroma, body, flavour and alcohol content can be varied to suit yourself.

Basic Processes of Brewing

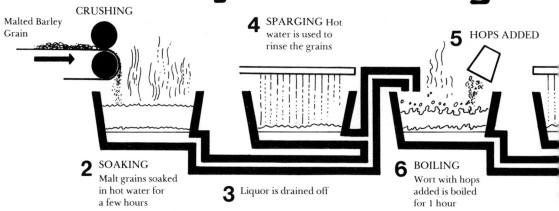

1 CRUSHING

Malted Barley Grain

2 SOAKING Malt grains soaked in hot water for a few hours

3 Liquor is drained off

4 SPARGING Hot water is used to rinse the grains

5 HOPS ADDED

6 BOILING Wort with hops added is boiled for 1 hour

It is believed that our word beer comes from the Anglo-Saxon word 'baere' which means barley. Barley has long been regarded as the most suitable grain for brewing beer. Wheat has been and — especially in Germany — sometimes still is used for brewing. In other places, especially in Africa, maize is used. These exceptions, however, tend to confirm the rule that malted barley is best for beer.

The brewer first cracks or crushes the hard malt grains between steel rollers. Then he soaks them in hot water for a few hours while the starch is converted into dextrins and maltose. The liquor, called wort, is drained off and the grains are sprayed or 'sparged' with more hot water to wash out the last traces of soluble substances. Hops are then added and the wort is boiled for an hour, both to extract the oils and resins from the hops and to precipitate the proteins. The wort is strained off, the hops are sparged, the wort is cooled to 59°F (15°C) and an active yeast is pitched into it.

Fermentation lasts only five days, during which the dirty froth is skimmed off several times. The young beer is then fined, primed and bottled. Although a few scientific controls have been implemented in this basic process, it has remained very much the same for the last four centuries.

Beer can be brewed at home in the manner just described and there are a good number of home brewers who follow this method. They claim that it makes the best beer and they adjust their ingredients and techniques to produce individual beers of their own choice.

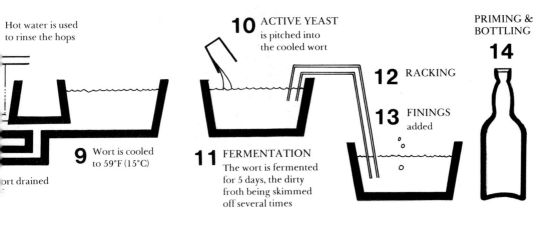

Hot water is used to rinse the hops

9 Wort is cooled to 59°F (15°C)

ort drained

10 ACTIVE YEAST is pitched into the cooled wort

11 FERMENTATION The wort is fermented for 5 days, the dirty froth being skimmed off several times

12 RACKING

13 FININGS added

PRIMING & BOTTLING

14

Fermentation vessel in a large brewery

Whilst not disagreeing with the validity of this claim, many other home brewers prefer to omit the lengthy mashing stage and use a malt extract prepared by commercial breweries especially for the domestic market. These extracts may be bought in the main styles of pale ale, bitter, brown ale and stout. All that they require is dilution to the recommended gravity, boiling with hops, straining, cooling, fermenting, and so on, as already described. This method saves the home brewer from the more difficult process and yet leaves a wide variety of options open. The beer can be made into any of the classical styles, adjusted to suit the brewer's palate, and may be bottled or casked as preferred. These beers are of excellent quality and, to many minds, as good as beers made from the mashed grains process.

The easiest method, however, is to brew from a prepared kit. Malt extracts are used mostly, adjusted to meet a given style and flavoured with hop oils and resins. All that the home brewer must do is dilute the extracts as instructed by the manufacturer, add a recommended amount of sugar, sprinkle on a yeast which is provided, and ferment the beer as already described. Some kits contain malt flour, grains and hops instead of the malt extract, but the principle is the same. These kits are extremely popular and are fine if you like the beer they produce, but they leave little or no room for variation to suit your own taste.

Brewing beer from kits is simplicity itself, takes very little time and often produces a beer as good as the less expensive pub beers and at a tenth of the price. Millions of beer kits are sold to produce from sixteen to forty pints of beer at a time, and recently, some very small kits to make only six pints have come on the market. Full, step-by-step instructions are issued with each kit and very little is needed in the way of equipment.

If you are brewing beer for the first time, it is a good way to start by making up two or three of these kits. You quickly get the knack of brewing and the confidence gained enables you to move on to other methods. Soon you will be brewing your own style of beer that you will rightly regard as being superior to its commercial equivalent. There is no doubt that the competent home brewer can produce a better beer than can be bought.

Equipment
for Home
Brewing

Kits

To make up a pre-prepared kit, only the very simplest equipment is needed. This can consist of nothing more than an ordinary polythene bag in a cardboard carton and some screw-stoppered beer bottles. A wooden spoon for stirring the malt extract and sugar in the water until it is dissolved, and a jug for filling the bottles, will be available in every kitchen. A large stew pan is needed for the dry kits but this, also, is part of the basic equipment of most kitchens.

An improvement on the bag is a suitably sized polythene bucket with a lid and produced especially for the home brewer and winemaker. They are made from high-density polythene and are fitted with a good lid and carrying handle. They are inert to acids and alkalis, light and easy to clean. They are usually in three sizes: 10 litre (2¼ gallons), 15 litres (3⅓ gallons), 25 litres (5½ gallons).

Also available is the 'Brew Bag'. This consists of a 27.5 litres (6 gallons) size, cube-shaped, medium-density polythene bag, fitted with a screw cap containing a plastic tap. The bag is held in shape by a collapsible metal framework. The great advantage of this piece of equipment is that after use it can be washed, dried and stored in a much smaller space than the polythene bins or buckets. Two bags are supplied so that the beer can be racked from one into the other when necessary. The second bag can also be used as a draught beer container simply by turning the bag on its side, tap down.

Poly-pins used for the commercial dispensing of sherry are also suitable after they have been washed and dried. They can sometimes be obtained for a few pence.

Both the Brew Bag and the Poly-pin are more suited to a bottom fermenting yeast, i.e. saccharomyces carlsbergensis than to the top-fermenting saccharomyces cerevisiae, since the latter needs skimming and the former does not.

Malt Extract and Hops Method

A polythene bin or bucket as already described is desirable in which to dissolve the malt and sugar and to ferment the beer, although a Brew Bag or Poly-pin could be used to ferment lager. A stainless steel stew pan or the like is needed for boiling the hops and wort. A long-handled, polypropylene or wooden spoon or paddle is needed for stirring and a siphon is better than a jug for racking and for filling bottles. Good use can be found for a polythene funnel, for a culinary thermometer and

Perhaps the simplest fermenter, a plastic bag inside a cardboard box

The Bag Boy brew bag in use

Home Brewing equipment

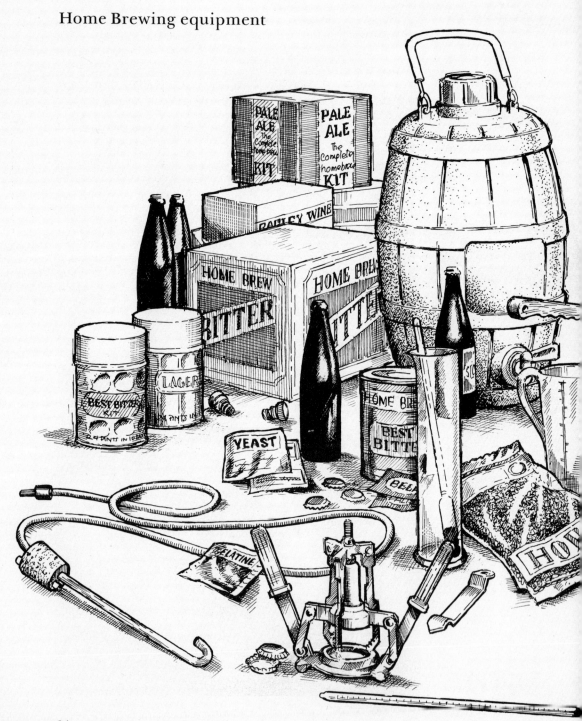

for an hydrometer. A nylon sieve or bag is also an aid in straining out the hops.

Whichever method is used, proper beer bottles are essential. They can be of the screw-stopper variety or those requiring a crown cap. Stoppers need new rubber rings from time to time. A new crown cap should be used every time a beer is bottled and a supply should always be kept available. A capping tool is needed and in the long run it pays to buy a two-handed instrument since this ensures a gas-tight seal. Some labels are also needed to indicate the type of beer in the bottle if more than one variety is stored at the same time. They also give your beer a professional finish.

The Grain Mash Method

Whenever possible, malt grain should always be bought crushed, but in the event of this not being possible, a means of crushing the grains is needed. A coarse mill or mincer will do, or a very hard surface such as marble or formica, in conjunction with a ceramic rolling pin or glass bottle. It is sufficient to crack open each grain and they must not be ground.

A mashing bin is required and this can be bought ready-made with a heater, thermostat and aerator. Alternatively, an ordinary polythene bin as previously described may be used in conjunction with an immersion heater and thermostat and a fish-tank bubbler. Some insulating material should be

A ready-made fermenter with immersion heater and lock

wrapped around the bin during mashing to prevent heat loss.

A boiler will subsequently be required for boiling the hops and malt liquor.

Other equipment, such as a hydrometer, thermometer and siphon, are also needed, since the fermentation and maturation processes are the same.

Apart from the Brew Bag and Poly-pin already mentioned, there are a variety of pressurised kegs available for maturing draught beers with or without carbon dioxide (CO_2) injectors.

General

If you intend to brew beer regularly, even in modest quantities, it is well worth investing in good equipment right from the start. It makes the work easier and safer and you are less likely to have faulty brews. When spread over the total quantity of beer produced, the cost is very small indeed.

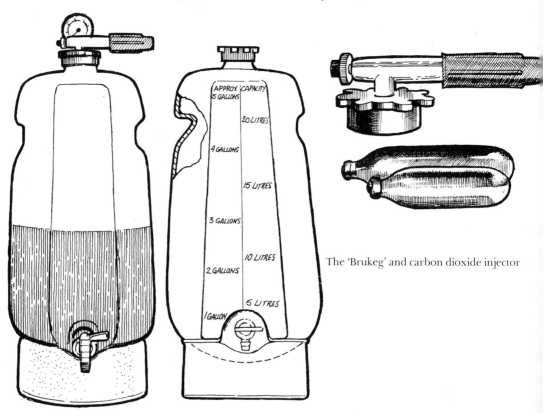

The 'Brukeg' and carbon dioxide injector

Ingredients for Home Brewing

Water

The importance of water in brewing has long been recognised. Soft water areas produce better mild ales, brown ales and stouts than tangy bitters. Hard water areas produce better bitters than other beers. Happily, we now know why, and whatever water you have — as long as it is pure and wholesome — it can be adjusted either way by the addition of certain salts. Home Brew shops sell packets of hardening salts that can be added to soft water when brewing bitter beers. The salts include calcium sulphate, magnesium sulphate and traces of other minerals. In hard water areas other salts may be added for the production of brown ales and stouts. These include sodium chloride, calcium chloride and calcium carbonate. The quantities required are minute. A simple rule-of-thumb guide is to add a pinch of gypsum to make one gallon of hard water or a pinch of table salt to make one gallon of soft water.

Rainwater is not recommended for brewing unless it is first filtered and boiled. Furthermore, it is usually extremely soft and needs the addition of mineral salts for all beers.

Malt

Barley grains are mostly used for malting, although some wheat is also used. In principle, the selected grains are soaked in water for some hours and then laid out several inches thick on the malting floor. It soon begins to grow in this warm, damp atmosphere and the maltster turns it over from time to time to keep the warmth and moisture even throughout the grain. After four or five days, tiny hair-like growths appear and within ten days the barley is ready for drying and roasting. During these ten days an enzyme called cytase causes the cellulose surrounding the starch to dissolve and changes the cellular structure of the grain. Insoluble proteins are converted into simpler and soluble nitrogenous substances.

The grain is next conveyed to a drying floor where it is dried with hot air before being roasted to stop further growth and development. Light roasting produces a 'pale' malt which is the basis for all brewing. Longer roasting or higher temperature roasting produces 'crystal' malt, and longer roasting still produces 'chocolate' or even 'black' malt. Crystal and chocolate malt impart colour and flavour as well as some starch to a mash. Black malt imparts only colour and flavour since all the starch has been caramelised. But in practice, modern machinery is now doing much of the maltster's work for him, and the method described above is slowly disappearing.

There are different varieties of barley and some varieties have been found to be more suitable for some beers than others. The commercial brewer will use different malts, then, for his different beers. The home brewer has no choice of barley grains although the better malt extracts take cognisance of these variations.

When malt is bought in quantity to obtain a reduction in price, it must be kept absolutely air-tight and free from humidity. Malt extract is less temperamental, but even this can deteriorate if left in a half-filled container for too long. The malt extract is made by the commercial mashing of malt grains as already described, and the wort is then boiled under pressure in a vacuum until the texture has become toffee-like and contains 80 per cent solids.

Adjuncts

Modern brewers use a variety of other ingredients to eke out the malt and improve the body, flavour and texture of different

Before germination

Beginning to shoot

Acrospires well developed

After light roasting

beers. The most commonly used adjuncts include roasted unmalted barley, flaked maize and rice, and wheat syrup. Not more than 10 per cent of the total ingredients used should be adjuncts otherwise the beer may be spoiled.

Hop garden in Kent

Hops

Before hops became the universal flavouring and preserving agent that it now is, nettles were widely used. The hop is a member of the nettle family. The climbing bines are cultivated to grow up strings to a wire frame that supports their weight. The hop flower is called a cone and is usually ripe and ready for harvesting about the 25 August. The cones are picked from the bines and dried in an oast-house to remove most of the moisture from them. They are then hand pressed into sacks and stored in very cool, dark conditions until required.

Different varieties of hops are grown for different kinds of beer. The delicately flavoured East Kent Golding hop is used for light ales and bitter beers, while the stronger flavoured Fuggle hop is used for brown ales and stouts. But other hops are used as well, and experiment goes on to find more suitable hops with better flavour and preservative qualities, more resistance to disease such as mildew and wilt, and heavier cropping. The Wye Challenger and Wye Northdown are the most important of the newly-developed varieties. Continental seedless hops are used for lager-type beers. Hops must be stored in dark and cool places and deteriorate if left open to the air, becoming dry and stale. Hop pellets sold in vapour-proof sachets avoid this danger.

Humulus lupulus
(hops)

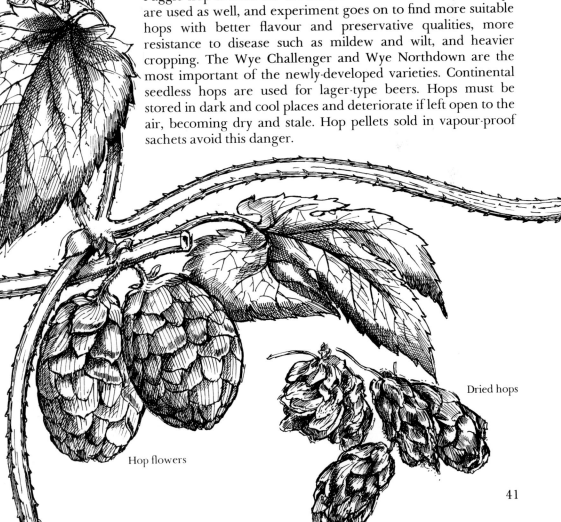

Dried hops

Hop flowers

Sugar

Originally, ale was made from malt alone and the gravity of the beers was obtained exclusively from the malt sugar — maltose. For the last hundred years or so, however, a proportion of the less expensive household sugar has been added to the wort to replace some of the more expensive malt. Commercially, a liquid sugar is used containing the immediately fermentable glucose. When brewing thousands of gallons of beer at a time, the risk of waiting even a few hours for fermentation to begin is too great. The possibility of infection can never be ignored. At home, the risk with a few gallons is far less and there appears to be no advantage in using the more expensive invert sugar or glucose syrup over ordinary household sugar. In any case, household sugar can easily be split into glucose and fructose by boiling it for twenty minutes with a little citric acid. The customary formula is 2lb sugar in one pint of water with a level teaspoonful of citric acid (1kg sugar in 0.62 litres of water with 5g citric acid).

Brown sugars are sometimes used to give colour to a beer.Golden syrup may also be used. Black treacle, although it colours a beer very well, leaves a caramel taste. Lactose is used to sweeten beer.

Yeast

That sweet liquids start to ferment and change their nature if left for a while has been known for perhaps ten thousand years. How soon fermentations were deliberately started is not known but it was probably some five thousand years ago. Leavened bread was well known in Biblical days, and fermented liquors, too.

What actually caused the fermentation was not known until the middle of the last century, and details of how it worked were not fully understood until this century. We now know that fermentation is caused by a single cell belonging to the plant world. It secretes a number of enzymes that act as catalysts and cause the conversion of one substance into others.

There are more than a thousand different yeasts, although very few of them are suitable for culinary use. For brewing and baking, a yeast called saccharomyces cerevisiae is used. However, this develops different strains, and home brewers should use a brewers' yeast rather than a bakers' yeast, since the latter will have something of a doughy flavour, while the former will have a beery flavour. Some strains can be

Oast houses in Kent

obtained from specific beers such as stout. The yeast cell absorbs some of the flavour of individual beers and imparts this to the next brew.

Being a plant cell the yeast needs nitrogen, and although barley is nitrogenous and the malt contains nitrogen, some home brewers add a little extra to their brews to ensure a full and vigorous fermentation. Ammonium phosphate or ammonium sulphate or a blend of both is used. Half a teaspoonful per gallon is ample (3g to 4.6 litres).

It is always advisable to pitch the yeast into the wort in a pre-activated form. This can be done by mixing the yeast with a dilute solution of malt, stirring or whisking it well to involve as much oxygen as possible, then leaving it loosely covered in a warm place for a few hours. In this way the yeast reproduces itself and forms a large colony of viable and active cells that will start attenuating the wort as soon as it is mixed in.

43

Brewing Beers at Home

Hygiene

Cleanliness is critical to the brewing of good beer at home. All equipment used should be washed clean in hot water and then sterilised with a sulphite solution. This can quickly be made by dissolving two crushed Campden tablets and a good pinch of citric acid in one pint of cold water. Carefully rinse all bins, bags, buckets, bottles, casks, stoppers, funnels, siphons, etc., with the solution and drain them dry. The solution may be poured from one vessel to another and will effectively sterilise each of them. Use the sterilised vessel as soon as possible to avoid it becoming re-contaminated.

This simple precaution will prevent many problems from ever arising. Keep fermenting beers covered to exclude airborne infection from spoilage micro-organisms such as vinegar bacteria. Once infected there is no alternative but to discard the brew. Bottles and casks must be securely sealed to keep in the gas and exclude the air, for these microbes flourish in the presence of air.

It also follows that all ingredients used should be fresh and of good quality. Stale, dirty and inferior ingredients will produce beers with unpleasant off-flavours that make the brew unpalatable. The savings in the cost of home-produced beers are so substantial that it pays to buy the very best ingredients available. Penny-pinching on ingredients is a false economy. Negligence in hygiene is inexcusable.

Hygiene: essential materials

From kits

Each of the many manufacturers of kits includes detailed in-structions with his kit and these should be carefully followed. There are two main types of kit, the dry and the wet. Dry kits consist of a bag of malt flour, a bag of hops, often mixed with a few malt grains, a bag of yeast and nutrient, and a bag of finings. All that you have to provide is some sugar and the requisite amount of water. Some packs call for quite a large amount of sugar in relation to the malt, and the resulting beers are sometimes thin and lacking in malty flavour, although adequately strong in alcohol.

The malt flour and sugar has to be dissolved in warm water, the bag of hops and grain must be emptied into a pan of water and boiled vigorously for up to one hour. After straining, the two liquors are mixed and topped up with cold water. When the temperature has fallen to 70°F (21°C), the yeast is added.

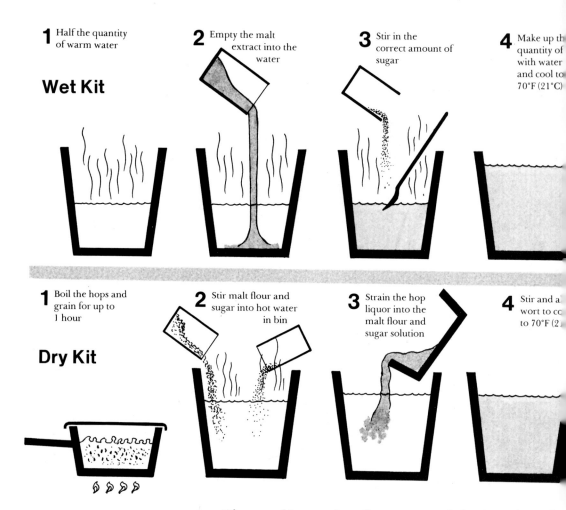

1 Half the quantity of warm water

2 Empty the malt extract into the water

3 Stir in the correct amount of sugar

4 Make up th quantity of with water and cool to 70°F (21°C)

Wet Kit

1 Boil the hops and grain for up to 1 hour

2 Stir malt flour and sugar into hot water in bin

3 Strain the hop liquor into the malt flour and sugar solution

4 Stir and a wort to co to 70°F (2

Dry Kit

The wet kits consist of a can or polythene sachet of toffee-like malt extract that has been adjusted to the style of the beer to be brewed. It contains the right amount of hop oils and resins and needs only sugar and water to be added. Some kits include a sachet of dried yeast and another of finings. Brewing from these kits could not be made more simple. Step-by-step instructions are printed on the labels. Newcomers to home brewing would be well advised to start with such a kit, preferably a small one.

The usual procedure is to dissolve the contents of the can in hot water, stir in the sugar, top up with cold water and, when the temperature has fallen to 70°F (21°C), to add the yeast. The bin is then covered, or the bag is closed, and left in a warm place for five days, the yeast head being skimmed off in between. Finings are then added and the beer is left for a day or two to clear. Bottling procedure is common to all beers.

5 Small amount of boiled water

6 Add a little malt

7 and yeast

8 Active yeast ready for use

9 Pitch in the active yeast

10 Set aside in a warm place for the fermentation period, skimming as required

11 Add finings

12 Allow to stand for a few days

13 Siphon off into a sterile vessel

14 Stir in priming sugar and bottle immediately

15 Store sealed bottles in cool place to mature

47

From malt extract and hops

When brewing beer from kits you have to take the beer as prepared for you. When brewing from malt extract and hops, you
have a degree of flexibility that enables you to brew a beer that
is exactly to your liking. It can be more malty or more hoppy or
stronger to suit your individual desires.

Malt flour may be used instead of malt extract. It is best
to buy only the quantity required for a single brew. Unless it is
kept completely air-tight, the flour rapidly absorbs moisture
from the air and deteriorates. Malt extract, on the other hand,
will keep quite well in a sealed container.

Hops, too, should preferably be freshly bought for each
brew, although the stockist could be out of your favourite hop
just when you wanted some. Make sure when you buy hops that
they have a fresh greeny-gold colour, feel sticky when rubbed
between the palms of your hands and smell clean and fresh.
Stale, brownish hops that look dry and faded should be
declined.

Another of the advantages of brewing from malt
extract and hops is that you can brew as little or as much as you
require, from one gallon to the maximum of your facilities.

The method is quite simple:

1. Pour some hot water into a sterilised bin half as large again
   as the quantity of beer being brewed.
2. Stir into this the required quantity of malt extract and
   sugar. If necessary, include some hardening salts or some
   table salt, depending on the water and the beer being
   brewed.
3. Boil the hops for at least 45 minutes and strain the liquor
   into the bin, stir well and top up with cold water.
4. When the temperature reaches 68°F (20°C) pitch an activated beer yeast suitable for the style being brewed.
5. Cover the bin to keep out dust and spoilage micro-
   organisms and leave the bin in a coolish place, around
   61°F (16°C) if possible for the period of fermentation.
6. Skim off the yeast heads on the second and third days and
   stir well.
7. When fermentation ends on or about the sixth day, cover
   the vessel tightly and leave it in a cool place for two days
   while the solid particles settle, undisturbed by the thermal
   currents induced by a warmer atmosphere.

Hops in good condition

8. Siphon the clearing beer into a clean vessel. If it is very muddy, stir in some proprietary brand beer finings and leave it for another two days. If it is only faintly hazy, stir in the priming sugar at the rate of not more than 1½oz per gallon (10g per litre).

9. Immediately bottle the beer into sterilised beer bottles, leaving some head room of about 1½in (4cm).

10. Seal each bottle perfectly and leave in a warmish place for a few days until bottle fermentation is complete. If the seal is not absolutely gas-tight under pressure, the carbon dioxide will slowly escape and the beer will be flat when poured. Ordinary corks as used for wine bottles are quite unsuitable.

11. Store the bottles, adequately labelled, in a cool place for several weeks while the beer matures. Contrary to common belief, well brewed beer that has been properly bottled will keep for over a year, improving all the time.

12. If a draught beer is required, it should be siphoned from its sediment into a pressure keg and primed as described. A

49

carbon dioxide injection is not normally required until a 5 gallon (22 litre) keg is half empty. The carbon dioxide from the priming provides adequate condition for the first two or three gallons drawn off, especially if this is within a relatively short time. The priming will be enough for the whole 5 gallons if the beer is all drawn off within a matter of hours at a party. Draught beer is rarely as bright as bottled beer. If you want it bright, fine it before putting it into cask, omit the priming sugar and use only a carbon dioxide injection to give it life, i.e. as in keg beer.

Variations to the basic ingredients may be used, such as the inclusion of some adjuncts, brown sugar, caramel, lactose and so on. Some suggestions are given in the recipes, but after a few brews, it is more fun to brew your beer to your own recipe.

Grain mash beers

Most of the malt sugar is extracted from pale malt and this should form the basis of every mash. Crystal, chocolate and black grains and adjuncts impart colour, body, aroma and flavour but little sugar. 1lb (450g) of pale malt grains yield a gravity of around 1.025 in one gallon of water. In metric terms this is 100g of pale malt in one litre of water.

The starch in the malt grains is converted into maltose and dextrin when soaked for several hours in hot water with a temperature somewhere between 130°F and 170°F (54°C and 77°C). In practice, most home brewers concentrate their mashing at or near 150°F (66°C). At the lower temperatures the maltose is extracted; at the higher temperatures some unfermentable insoluble dextrins are also produced which give body and sweetness to a beer. In some beers this is undesirable.

How to mash the grains has already been described on page 35. After a period of two hours, the wort should be checked to see whether all the starch has yet been converted to maltose. A tablespoonful of wort is placed in a white saucer and a few drops of tincture of iodine are added. If the colour of the wort darkens, then some starch still remains and mashing must continue until the colour of the wort remains unchanged by the iodine test. Further checks should be made at half-hourly intervals.

After straining off the wort and sparging the grains with hot water, any sugar is stirred in, hops are added, and the wort must be boiled vigorously for one hour in a covered pan. It is then left, still covered, for half an hour to cool before straining

Good simple fare

out and sparging the hops with tepid water. The wort is then topped up with cold water to reach the required quantity and cooled as quickly as possible to around 59°F (15°C).

An activated beer yeast is then pitched and fermentation is conducted in the same way as described for malt extract beers. At the priming stage, some home brewers use a solution of malt extract instead of sugar, making allowance for the 20 per cent water content of the extract. Others save some of the original wort, bottled and sealed whilst still hot and prime their beers with this. One quart at specific gravity (s.g.) 1.040 is sufficient to add to 4¾ gallons, making up to 5 gallons, provided the bulk has been fully fermented. This is one litre in twenty if you are working in metric. The idea behind this is to obtain better head retention.

Bottling and casking is the same as already described — similarly, the period for maturation (see page 49).

Serving beer

When suitably matured, most beers are best served cool rather than cold, except lager, which is best served cold rather than chilled. All beers look best in a plain, clear glass with a short stem attached to a base. In such a glass one can enjoy the beauty of a creamy head, translucent clarity and a continuing bead of bubbles. In metal and ceramic tankards, this joy is denied.

Most beers can be enjoyed on their own and without food, but they do make superb companions to cold food of many kinds. The outstanding accompaniment to all beers is a plate of crusty bread, butter, English cheeses and the stronger salads such as spring onion, radish, watercress, and the like.

Beer is not as often used in cooking as it deserves to be and merits wider recognition from cooks. Try sausages poached in beer, for example. Simple recipes with simple foods are much enhanced with a little beer in the ingredients instead of water.

There are few people who do not enjoy a glass of good beer. It appeals to women as much as to men, to the old as well as to the young, and to the rich as well as to the poor. Different people, however, do have different preferences and the home brewer has the opportunity to produce — and keep readily available — a wide range of beers appealing to every palate.

Recipes
for
Beers

Kits

All beer kits are made to specific styles such as bitter, brown, or stout. Readers are recommended to follow the manufacturer's instructions precisely. If you are not completely satisfied with the result, try the same style from a different manufacturer. Each has his own idea as to what the style should be like. Experience has shown that attempts to vary kits are not very successful and they are best made up as supplied.

Malt extract and hops

Use only Imperial or only metric measures throughout your brew. Never use some Imperial and some metric, since this may throw the recipe out of balance.

Basic bitter

1lb (500g) plain malt extract
8oz (250g) granulated white sugar
1oz (30g) Golding hops
8 pints (5 litres) water
Beer yeast

1 MIX malt extract, sugar and 1 quart boiling water in fermenting bin

2 COOL 1 cup of wort and add the yeast

3 BOIL the hops for ¾ hour

1. Empty the malt extract into a suitable bin, add the sugar, pour on one quart of boiling water and stir until the malt and sugar are dissolved. Remember to rinse out the jar or can so that no malt is wasted.

2. Take out a cupful of the wort, pour it into a jug or basin, cool it rapidly, add the yeast, stir it well and leave it in a warm place to activate.

3. Place the hops in a large pan, pour on a quart of the cold water and wet the hops thoroughly. Cover the pan, bring the water to the boil and keep it there for three-quarters of an hour. Remove the pan from the heat and leave it for fifteen minutes to cool. A pressure cooker may be used instead for fifteen minutes at 15lb (6.8kg) pressure.

4. Strain the hop liquor on to the malt liquor, press the hops dry and add two quarts of cold water. Cover the bin and leave the wort to cool to 68°F (20°C).

5. Pitch the activated yeast into the bin of wort, give it a good stir, cover the bin and leave it in an even temperature, around 68°F (20°C).

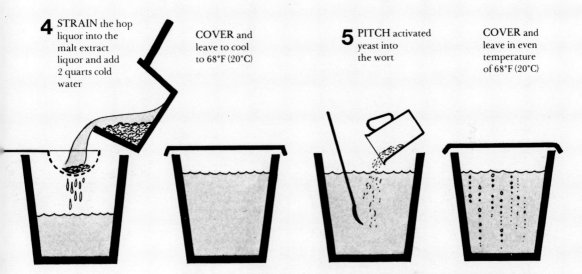

4 STRAIN the hop liquor into the malt extract liquor and add 2 quarts cold water

COVER and leave to cool to 68°F (20°C)

5 PITCH activated yeast into the wort

COVER and leave in even temperature of 68°F (20°C)

6. Next day, skim off all the froth and stir the wort a few times. Repeat this on each of the next two days, but keep the bin covered in the meantime. Leave the fermentation to finish undisturbed for a further three days.

7. Move the bin to as cool a place as you can find and leave it there for two days while the solid particles settle.

8. Carefully lift the bin on to a suitable work surface without disturbing the sediment.

9. Wash and sterilise nine beer bottles of the one-pint size and have handy the sterilised screw stoppers with good rubber rings or crown caps and a crimping tool.

10. Siphon the beer into the bottles until the level is 1½in (4cm) from the top. By carefully tilting the bin, it will be possible to fill the nine bottles and discard only the pasty sediment.

11. Into each bottle, funnel one scant level 5ml spoonful of caster sugar. This quantity is critical. Do not be generous. Scrape each spoonful with a flat-bladed knife to ensure that the quantity is equal for every bottle. Too much sugar will cause too great a gush when the bottle is opened. It is better to use less rather than more.

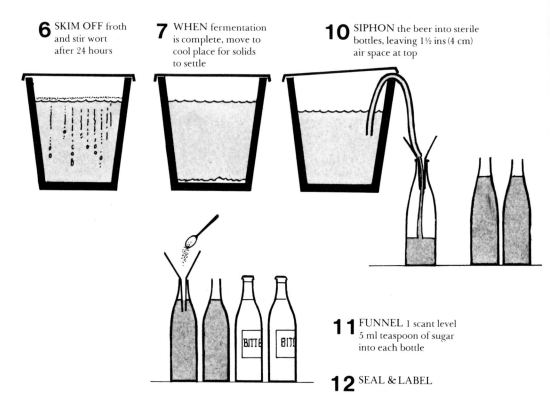

6 SKIM OFF froth and stir wort after 24 hours

7 WHEN fermentation is complete, move to cool place for solids to settle

10 SIPHON the beer into sterile bottles, leaving 1½ ins (4 cm) air space at top

11 FUNNEL 1 scant level 5 ml teaspoon of sugar into each bottle

12 SEAL & LABEL

12. Seal each bottle securely, label it with the style and date and shake it well to dissolve the sugar.

13. Leave the bottles in a warm place for a few days until the sugar is fermented, then move the bottles to a cool store for three weeks. Stand the bottles upright so that the sediment settles on the bottom.

14. Before serving, cool the beer in the refrigerator for a short while and prepare suitable glasses. Handle each bottle carefully so as not to disturb the sediment. Unseal the bottle and pour the beer down the side of each glass without reverting the bottle to the upright. In this manner all the beer can be poured with perfect clarity and only the pasty sediment is left in the bottle.

15. The beer should have a good aroma, a clean, hoppy, malty flavour and plenty of satisfaction. A creamy head will develop and then fade, but beads of condition will rise in each glass for from twenty to thirty minutes — if the beer is not drunk long before then!

Variations

This basic recipe and method can be varied in many different ways to suit your preference.

1. Use brown sugar instead of white to darken the colour and give a hint of caramel to the flavour.
2. Replace the sugar with Golden Syrup. It subtly varies the colour, flavour and alcohol content.
3. Make a mild beer by omitting the sugar and using only three-quarters of the hops.
4. Add a handful of dry hops to the wort after the final skimming. This increases the tangy flavour, especially in hard water areas.
5. Make a brown ale by adding 4oz (125g) cracked crystal malt grains to the hops before boiling and 1oz (30g) lactose to only 4oz (125g) brown sugar instead of the white sugar. This produces a just slightly-sweet, dark beer that is very enjoyable.
6. In addition to the crystal grains just mentioned, boil 2oz (60g) whole black grains with the hops and use a different variety — Fuggles instead of Goldings. This produces an excellent stout for those who do not enjoy totally dry beers. Of course, the lactose may be omitted if you so prefer. Alternatively, the quantity may be quadrupled if you would like to make a milk stout.
7. Boil 4oz (120g) flaked oatmeal with the hops and grains just mentioned to make an oatmeal stout.

The variations are endless and these seven are but examples to show you the way to make experiments for yourself. When you feel that you have sufficient confidence, brew in larger quantities and produce draught beers. Remember that draught beers do not keep as well as bottled beers and should be consumed within a week or so after broaching the pressure cask. The beers produced from this basic recipe for malt extract and hops will keep in bottle for at least a year — improving for much of that time.

Grain Mash Beers

It is assumed that experience will have been gained by first making up a few kits and then brewing some malt extract and hop beers, before grain mash beers are attempted. These recipes, therefore, are more sophisticated. However, they may also be varied to suit your taste, using a little more or less or omitting or substituting certain ingredients. As set out, these recipes have produced enjoyable and satisfying beers — clear, clean and tasty.

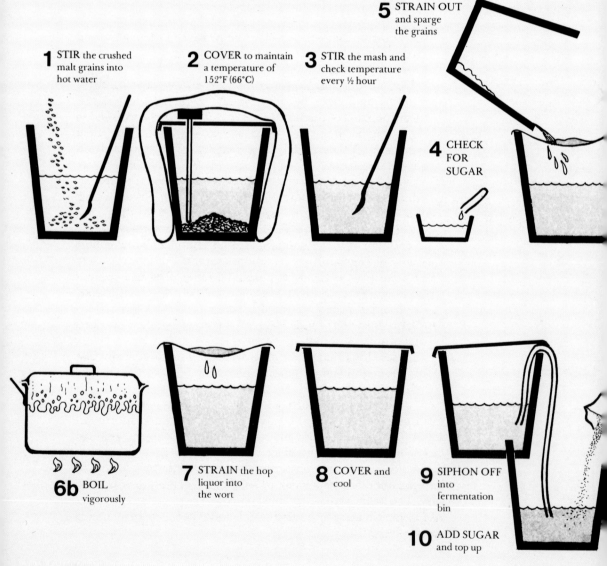

5 STRAIN OUT and sparge the grains

1 STIR the crushed malt grains into hot water

2 COVER to maintain a temperature of 152°F (66°C)

3 STIR the mash and check temperature every ½ hour

4 CHECK FOR SUGAR

6b BOIL vigorously

7 STRAIN the hop liquor into the wort

8 COVER and cool

9 SIPHON OFF into fermentation bin

10 ADD SUGAR and top up

Bitter Beer

4lb (2kg) crushed pale malt grains
2oz (60g) Golding hops
Beer finings
Sugar and water to make up to 16½ pints (10¼ litres) at an
    original gravity of 1.044.
Beer yeast

6a ADD the hops
and finings

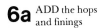

1. Heat three-quarters of the water to 167°F (75°C) and pour it
   into a suitable mashing bin. Slowly sprinkle on the grains,
   stirring the whole time.
2. If available, fit an immersion heater and thermostat set at
   152°F (66°C). Cover the bin and insulate it well.
3. Stir the mash every half hour to encourage the extraction
   of the maltose and to prevent the mash from setting into a
   porridge. If there is no thermostat, check the temperature
   and, if necessary, raise it to 152°F (66°C). This temperature
   should be maintained the whole of the mashing period.
4. After two hours, remove a sample of the wort and check
   with a few drops of iodine to see whether all the starch has
   been converted into sugar. If the wort turns blue or
   darkens, continue mashing for another half hour before
   checking again.
5. When all the starch has been converted, strain out the
   grains and rinse them in 2 pints (1 litre) of hot water. Add
   this to the wort and discard the grains.
6. Add the hops and finings, cover and boil the wort
   vigorously for an hour.

1 PREPARE
starter bottle

7. Leave for half an hour, then strain out the hops and rinse
   them in a quart of warm water. Add this to the wort and
   discard the hops.
8. Cover the wort and cool to 68°F (20°C) as quickly as you
   can.
9. Siphon the wort into a fermentation bin, discarding any
   lees.
10. Top up with cold water and stir in caster sugar until a total
    quantity of 16½ pints or 10¼ litres, with a gravity of 1.044 is
    obtained.
11. Make a starter bottle from half a pint (0.3 litre) of wort and
    the yeast.

12 Remove and set aside 1 pint of wort

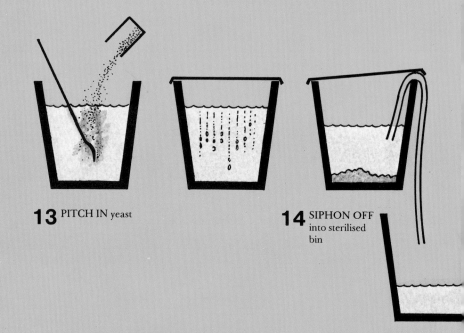

13 PITCH IN yeast

14 SIPHON OFF into sterilised bin

12. Remove one pint of wort (0.6 litre) and store in a sterilised and sealed bottle in the refrigerator for subsequent use as priming.
13. Pitch the yeast, stir well, ferment and skim as already described for malt extract and hop beer.
14. Move the beer to a cool place for two days and then siphon into a clean container, discarding about half a pint (0.3 litre) of pasty deposit.
15. Add the one pint (0.6 litre) of unfermented wort, stir gently until it is evenly distributed, then bottle it immediately and seal well.
16. Keep the bottles in a warm place for a few days' fermentation, then store upright in a cool place for at least four weeks.
17. Serve this beer as already described for malt extract and hop beer. It should have an equally clean, hoppy, malty flavour with that extra something, as well as good head retention and condition. **Note:** In soft water areas, hardening salts should be added to the water at the very outset. The proprietor of your local Home Brew shop will supply you and advise on the quantity to use in relation to the degree of softness of your water.

Brown Ale

3lb (1.5kg) crushed pale malt grains
8oz (250g) crushed crystal malt grains
2oz (60g) whole black malt grains
1¼oz (35g) Fuggle hops
4oz (125g) lactose
Beer finings
Sugar and water to make up to 16½ pints (10¼ litres) at
an original gravity of 1.038
Beer yeast
Note: Soft water is preferred. In hard water areas add half
a level teaspoonful of table salt.

15 STIR IN priming and bottle immediately

1. Mash the grains as already described but at the lower
temperature of 146°F (63°C).
2. Add the lactose with the priming liquor, making sure that it
is thoroughly dissolved.
3. Serve at room temperature.

Dry Stout

3lb (1.5kg) crushed pale malt grains
8oz (250g) crushed crystal malt grains
8oz (250g) whole black malt grains
8oz (250g) malt extract
4oz (125g) roasted barley grains
1½oz (45g) Fuggle hops
Beer finings
Sugar and water to make up to 16½ pints (10¼ litres) at an
original gravity of 1.048
Stout yeast
Note: Soft water is preferred. In hard water areas add half a
level teaspoonful of table salt.

1. Mash all the grains at 148°F (64°C).
2. Add the malt extract to the wort prior to the hops.
3. Serve at room temperature.

Milk Stout

Ingredients as above, but omit the roasted barley grains, thus
softening the flavour. Adjust the starting gravity to 1.040 and
add 8oz (250g) lactose with the priming. Serve at room
temperature.

Barley Wine

2lb (1kg) crushed pale malt grains
4oz (125g) crushed crystal malt grains
4oz (125g) malt extract
2oz (60g) wheat syrup
1oz (30g) Golding hops
½ tsp (3g) citric acid
½ tsp (3g) diammonium phosphate
Beer finings
Brown sugar and water to 8½ pints (5¼ litres) at an
    original gravity of 1.080.
Beer yeast and champagne wine yeast

Note: Hard water is preferred.

1. Mash the two grains at a temperature of 154°F (67°C).
2. Add the malt extract and wheat syrup.
3. Boil with the hops and finings.
4. Add sugar and adjust quantity.
5. Add an activated beer yeast.
6. When S.G. 1.030 is reached, stir in the acid, nutrient and
   activated wine yeast, pour into a fermentation jar, fit an air-
   lock and ferment down to 1.004.
7. Siphon into half-pint bottles, seal well, and leave
   in a warm place for a further week.
8. Store in a cool place for at least six months. Serve
   at room temperature in 5oz glasses.

Lager

3lb (1.5kg) crushed lager malt grains
1lb (500g) crushed pale malt grains
1oz (30g) Hallertau or Saaz hops
Beer finings
Sugar and water to make up to 16½ pints (10¼ litres) with an
    original gravity of 1.052
Carlsbergensis yeast

Note: Soft water is preferred. In hard water areas add a large
pinch of salt.

1. Mash at 140°F (60°C).
2. Boil with hops and finings.

3. Add sugar and adjust quantity.
4. Save one pint (0.6 litre) for priming.
5. Pitch an activated yeast.
6. As Carlsbergensis is a bottom fermenting yeast, skimming is not necessary. The wort should be fermented in glass jars fitted with airlocks.
7. Leave the jars in a warm place until a good fermentation is evident, then move the jars to a cooler place, around 50-54°F (10-12°C) until fermentation is complete. A slow fermentation is preferred.
8. Rack into a clean vessel, add the priming wort, bottle and seal immediately.
9. Leave the bottles in a warm place for three days and then move them to a cool store for three months.
10. Serve lager cool to cold.

UNUSUAL BEERS

Cock Ale

1 gallon (4.5 litres) of medium-hopped, malt wort of
  S.G. 1.044
Carcase bones, wing tips, tail, neck and serving scraps of
  a plainly roasted chicken
½ pint (0.3 litre) of dry white wine

1. Crush the bones and place them with all the chicken pieces in a bowl containing the wine. Cover and leave in a cool larder or refrigerator for 24 hours.
2. Pitch an active yeast into the wort, cover it and leave it in a warm place to start a vigorous fermentation.
3. Next day, strain the wine into the wort, place all the chicken pieces and bones in a coarse nylon or muslin bag and

suspend this in the wort. Replace the cover and continue the fermentation. The presence of some fat from the chicken will inhibit the formation of a frothy head but will not stop the fermentation.

4. After three days, withdraw, drain and discard the bag of chicken and continue the fermentation to the finish. This will take two or three days longer than usual.
5. Clear, bottle, prime, seal and mature for at least one month.

This is a well-tried adaptation of the old country habit of killing, plucking, cleaning and flaying an old cockerel and adding the broken bones and flesh to a barrel of fermenting beer. The result is a very fine beer, well worth brewing.

Honey Beer

1lb (500g) brown honey
½oz (15g) Fuggle hops
¼oz (7g) citric acid
1 tsp (5g) ammonium phosphate
1 gallon (5 litres) water
Brewers' yeast

1. Boil the hops in half the water for three-quarters of an hour, then strain into a bin.
2. Stir in the honey and top up to the five-litre or one-gallon mark with cold water.
3. Stir in the acid, phosphate, and active yeast and ferment out.
4. Clear, bottle, prime, seal and mature for one or two weeks.

Treacle Ale

Replace the brown honey in the previous recipe with 1lb (500g) of black treacle. The other ingredients and method are unchanged.

These are adaptations of old recipes once made by people in hard times, especially in Scotland. They were regarded as nourishing drinks and were sometimes added to porridge instead of milk. Without acid and phosphate, fermentation would have been poor and the resulting drink would have been sweet, but not very alcoholic.

Fruit Ales

Before the days of tea, coffee, cocoa and the many other beverages available today, country people used to flavour some

of their ales with fruits and berries of various kinds. Sometimes hops would be included, but more often not.

Elderberries. 8oz per gallon of beer or 250g per five litres. Pick black, ripe elderberries free from their stalks and boil them for half an hour. Strain them into the wort, then ferment and finish in the usual way. An alternative to stout.

Blackberries. 1lb per gallon of beer or 500g per five litres. Stalk, wash and crush the blackberries and add them to the wort. Ferment and finish in the usual way. Very popular.

Raspberries. 8oz per gallon of light ale or 250g per five litres. Treat in the same way as for blackberries.

Blackcurrants. 8oz per gallon of strong ale or 250g per five litres. Strig, wash and crush the blackcurrants, then add to the wort.

Rowanberries. 1lb per gallon of wort or 500g per five litres. Stalk, wash, crush and boil the berries for half an hour, then strain into the wort. Makes a bitter beer. Use no hops.

Nettles. 2lb per gallon of mild wort or 1kg per five litres. Gather young nettles and tops of older plants. Boil for half an hour and strain on to the malt. Use no hops.

Ginger Beer

1½oz (45g) bruised root ginger
1lb (450g) white sugar
1 gallon (4.5 litres) water
½oz (15g) cream of tartar
2 lemons (rind and juice only)
½oz (15g) granulated yeast

Thinly pare the lemon rinds, place them in a suitable vessel with the bruised ginger, cream of tartar and sugar. Pour on boiling water and stir until the sugar is dissolved, then cover the vessel and leave to cool. Add the lemon juice and yeast granules, replace the cover, and ferment in a warm place for three days. Siphon into sterilised beer bottles, leaving 2in (5cm) head space. Seal and store in a cool larder or refrigerator for four days and serve cold.

At this stage the ginger beer tastes sweet and is nicely gassy. If kept too long it will become stronger, very gassy and dry. An alternative method is to ferment out, prime as for ordinary beer and sweeten with saccharin. This prevents any possibility of burst bottles in hot weather.

Cider making~Past and present

According to Biblical tradition, Eve tempted Adam with an apple in the Garden of Eden, although we do not know precisely where this was or when. We do know, however, that in England the apple was greatly respected by the Ancient Druids. The wild apple must surely have formed part of man's early diet. Making a fermented drink from its juice could not have remained unknown for long.

The old Hebrew word 'shekar' is usually translated as meaning a strong drink. It is also thought to have been the origin of the Latin word 'sicera', meaning the beverage produced by fermenting the juice of apples. The old French word 'sidre', meaning cider as we know it, probably came from the Latin word.

Cider — a gift from the Romans?

Possibly cider was a gift to Britain from the Romans. The climate not being hospitable to the growing of grapes for wine and the abundant apples growing wild, may well have given ideas to the Romans. It would not have been beyond their wit to attempt to make a wine from the juice in the same way as they had seen wine made from grape juice at home in Italy.

There is evidence that cider making was practised long before the Norman Conquest, for St Brieuc, buried in the Parish Church at Braunston, near Barnstaple in North Devon, took cider apple trees with him when he visited Normandy in the sixth century.

The Norman Conquest

The Norman Conquest, no doubt, also gave a fillip to cider making, since many of the soldiers were accustomed to drinking cider at home in Normandy. The first documentary evidence, however, is not recorded until 1205, and then in Norfolk. Towards the end of that century, there is also documentary evidence of cider making in Kent, Surrey, Sussex and the Home Counties generally, as well as in the West Country.

Cider was well known in Chaucer's day and, in the centuries that followed, was certainly made on the feudal estates along with mead and ale.

The seventeenth century

In 1676, John Worlidge, gentleman, wrote 'A treatise on cider and other wines extracted from fruits growing in this Kingdom'. His book was nobly entitled *Vinetum Britannicum*. In his introduction he wrote as follows: 'The cider made in Herefordshire, Gloucestershire and Worcestershire, being in great quantities carried to London and several other places of the Kingdom and sold at a very high rate, and valued above the wines of France, partly from its own excellency and partly from the deterioration of the French wines which suffer in their exportation and from the sophistication and adulterations they receive from those that trade in them'.

Worlidge also wrote about wine and believed that 'wine from the grape is the richest drink this world affords'. He also went on to say that 'for our climate, cider, perry, cherry and gooseberry wines, etc., etc., are better'.

On reading his book, it is clear that John Worlidge was an authority on cider and advocated some three hundred years ago methods still in use today. He invented a cider mill for crushing apples and depicted presses that may still be in use. He recommended the scalding of all containers in case 'they ferment the cider too violently and make it acid'. The spoilage organisms that we know of, he referred to as 'wild spirits', and he knew that they entered cracks in casks and existed in unscalded vessels. He used brimstone for sterilising and he preferred the newly-invented corks to glass stoppers or mutton fat seals. Worlidge also recommended the storage of casks in sand to maintain an even temperature during maturation. He illustrated the siphon and knew the benefits of racking. He knew, too, of the yeast used in baking bread and brewing beer, but preferred the yeasts that occurred naturally on the fruits.

Throughout his book, Worlidge frequently uses the word wine when specifically referring to cider. To him, at least, cider was the wine of the apple. This gives support to a belief still existent, that the old vineyards were in fact cider apple orchards and that the produce of these vineyards was not wine made from the juice of the grape, but wine, i.e. cider, made from the juice of the apple. Perhaps there were some of each.

Old cider
press

Cider apple orchard

The decline of cider

The seventeenth and eighteenth centuries were the Golden Age of cider making. With the advent of tea, coffee and cocoa, and the drift of the people from the countryside to the towns, cider making and drinking slowly declined. The orchards were neglected and only a few farmers kept the craft alive.

More on cider making

Then, in the 1890s, it was realised by a few entrepreneurs that cider manufacture could be profitable if it was made and distributed on a wide scale to the towns. New varieties of cider apple trees were brought over from Normandy and, later, the National Fruit and Cider Institute was established at Long Ashton, near Bristol.

As a result of the work at the Institute, new varieties of tree have been developed. They are smaller and more compact than their predecessors and can be mechanically pruned. They give a much greater yield to the acre and the fruit quality, too, has been much improved, being juicier and more flavoursome. Each year more land is being planted with these new trees. One firm alone is planting as many as 100,000 trees that they have developed in their own nursery.

Meanwhile, apples of any kind — dessert varieties such as Cox's Orange Pippin and Worcester Pearmain, culinary varieties such as Bramleys and Derbys, and cider varieties such as Yarlington Mill, Dabinette and Michelin are all washed, crushed, pressed and fermented into cider by the millions of gallons. Concentrated cider apple juice is imported from Normandy to blend in with the home grown apple juice and to help meet the increasing market requirement for good, clean, tasty cider.

Modern technology produces sound cider as a matter of course. The craftsman's skill in blending produces different ciders to suit all palates. New methods of marketing and distribution create and satisfy a demand all the year round.

With the reawakened interest in cider and the development of home brewing stems a desire to know how to make a cider in the home. Its fruity, mouth-cleaning, thirst-satisfying qualities can now be enjoyed by anyone, but those people with some equipment and knowledge can also enjoy the ancient satisfaction of having made it themselves.

Some of the manufacturers and distributors of concentrated beer worts, malt extracts and grape concentrates now offer concentrated cider juice as well. It is widely available in a can sufficient to make up into 2 gallons (9 litres) of cider. Yeast is supplied together with detailed instructions. All you have to provide is a little sugar and the water. The method is simplicity itself and takes but a few minutes. Fermentation is straightforward, screw-stoppered mineral water bottles are recommended and maturation takes only three months. This is cider the easy way and well worth following once or twice until you feel confident enough to make cider from apples.

Basic Principles of Cider Making

Dessert apples by their very nature contain more sugar than acid and tannin. Culinary apples contain more acid than sugar or tannin. A balanced cider, however, needs not only a strong flavour but also acid, sugar and tannin, and these are found in a blend of cider apples. They can be divided into the following groups: Sweet, Bitter Sweet, Bitter Sharp and Sharp. Cider makers like to use about 75 per cent sweet and bitter sweet apples and 25 per cent bitter sharp and sharp apples to make a balanced cider. In practice this is not always possible and so the finished ciders are blended to make a variety of slightly different ciders to meet as many different tastes as possible.

The most popular cider apple varieties today are: Chisel-Jersey, Coates-Jersey, Dabinette, Michelin, Stembridge-Jersey and Yarlington Mill. A few older varieties are still being used in places but they are dying out, Yarlington Mill being the best of them. The Jersey varieties represent the new strains recently developed, and Dabinette and Michelin are the imported strains.

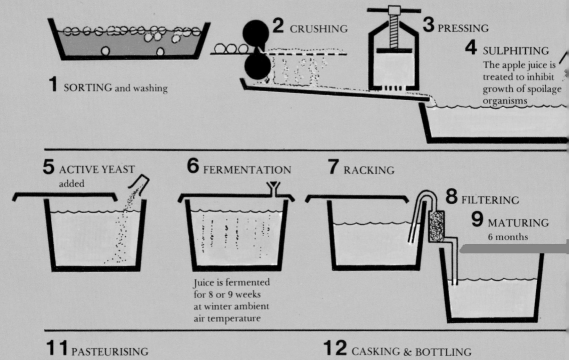

1 SORTING and washing

2 CRUSHING

3 PRESSING

4 SULPHITING
The apple juice is treated to inhibit growth of spoilage organisms

5 ACTIVE YEAST added

6 FERMENTATION

Juice is fermented for 8 or 9 weeks at winter ambient air temperature

7 RACKING

8 FILTERING

9 MATURING
6 months

11 PASTEURISING

12 CASKING & BOTTLING

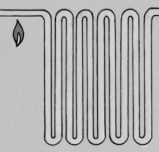

Cider is raised to 167°F (75°C) very quickly and then cooled, killing any ferments or germs without harming the cider

Cider apples are hard to come by for the vast majority of home cider makers, since there are insufficient to meet the demands of the cider factories. When all the new trees are in full production, however, it may be possible to buy them from the growers, either whole or in concentrate form.

Apples used for cider making have to be fully ripe so that they contain as much sugar as possible. It is customary not to gather them from the ground until several days after they have fallen from the tree and so have had time to mellow. They are then collected mechanically and taken in lorry-loads to the cider factory. Here they are tipped into a deep trough of water and thoroughly washed. The sound apples float on the surface of the water and can easily be scooped up by a conveyor belt fitted with prongs. As they are lifted up they are rinsed in fresh water. Badly damaged and rotten apples fill with water and sink to the bottom of the trough with the dirt.

The good apples are then mechanically crushed and pressed in a continuous cycle to extract as much juice as possible. About 170 gallons of juice is extracted from 1 ton of apples. In simpler terms, this is 1 gallon of juice from 13½lb of apples or 10 litres from 13.5kg. The average resultant specific gravity of the juice is usually around 1.044, but can vary from 1.012 to 1.064.

To prevent oxidation and to inhibit the growth of spoilage organisms, the juice is immediately sulphited at the rate of 100 p.p.m., equivalent to two Campden tablets per gallon or 5 litres. All vessels are sterilised before use and are kept closely covered when filled.

O CIDERS ARE BLENDED

A day later, an activated yeast culture is added. It is obtained in a tiny phial from the Cider Institute and developed through various quantities until the colony is large enough to ferment the quantity of juice to be made into cider. The variety of yeast used is saccharomyces cerevisiae uvarum. This is a very close relative of saccharomyces cerevisiae elipsoideus — more generally known as wine yeast. A general-purpose strain of elipsoideus may be used, but slightly better results may be obtained from a champagne strain.

Apple juice normally contains sufficient nitrogen for the yeast, and the pectin content of the juice tends to reduce adequately during maturation by the action of the natural enzymes always present in the skin of the apples.

Fermentation is conducted quite slowly at the normal late autumn and winter air temperatures in the West of England. Because of the large quantities fermented at a time — 70,000 gallons or more in a single vat — several degrees of heat are produced by the fermentation itself. This is just sufficient to keep the fermentation moving slowly throughout January and February, for it usually takes eight or nine weeks to complete. The vessel is sealed and fitted with a gas release valve so that no contamination of the cider can occur. It is protected by the carbon dioxide given off by the fermentation.

When all the sugar has been converted to alcohol and there is no further movement, the cider is racked from its sediment, filtered, centrifuged and matured for six months. It is then blended and, if necessary, sweetened to produce the style required. Then it is flash pasteurised and bottled or casked immediately prior to despatch. Most ciders are made for early drinking after despatch, but bottled ciders will keep in good condition for several months longer. Draught cider, however, will keep for only three or four weeks in its sealed cask before beginning to deteriorate. Once broached, draught cider will keep in good condition for only a few days.

Stronger ciders, and those containing more acid and tannin, will keep and improve for one or two years. Some dry ciders are often bottled when the S.G. is 1.002. The fermentation continues slowly in the bottle and gives it a natural condition or sparkle when poured. Sparkling cider is made by impregnating it with carbon dioxide at the bottling stage. The cost of using either of the methods for making sparkling wine are too expensive for the cider industry. The difference in the quality in relation to the extra cost is not considered to be worthwhile.

Cider is at its best when served cool rather than cold or at room temperature. It is as strong as and often stronger than beer, but less strong than imported table wines. Good cider has a mild and gentle flavour, although smelling and tasting of bitter sweet apples. It makes an excellent thirst-quenching drink at any time, accompanies light foods, picnics and snacks superbly well, and enhances the flavour of many cooked dishes when used in place of water or stock.

Scrumpy

This is a natural, unsophisticated cider, usually made in relatively small quantities by a farmer and sold to the local community. There are rarely any attempts to blend a range of ciders to produce a distinctive or even balanced whole. Furthermore, the apples used are the apples that the farmer has in his orchard and are not specially selected.

Some scrumpies are well made in sterilised vessels, others are less successful. Too often the cider is made in the traditional manner of local forebears, without regard to modern hygiene and technology. As a result, some scrumpies are oxidised or acetified or tainted with an off-flavour that proper care could have prevented.

Equipment for Cider Making

Cider making is not as difficult in the home as might at first be thought. The kitchen sink with its abundant supply of cold water will do very well for washing the fruit and sorting out the good from the bad. There are some excellent fruit crushers on the market that will handle 50lb (22kg) of apples at a time. They look like a wheelbarrow sitting on top of a mangle and work on the same principle. For a bucketful of apples at a time you can buy a stainless steel blade on a shaft that fits into the chuck of an electric drill. The shaft is passed through a polythene lid of a bin filled with apples and connected to the drill. The lid is fitted to the bin and held tight. The drill is switched on and the blade moves up and down in the bin. Very soon the apples are most efficiently crushed, the bin is emptied, filled with more apples and the process repeated until all the apples are crushed.

A wooden crusher can also be bought or made from a baulk of oak timber some 4in x 4in x 10in (10cm x 10cm x 25cm), attached to a broom handle. A layer of apples is placed in a bin and stomped with the crusher. It is very effective and

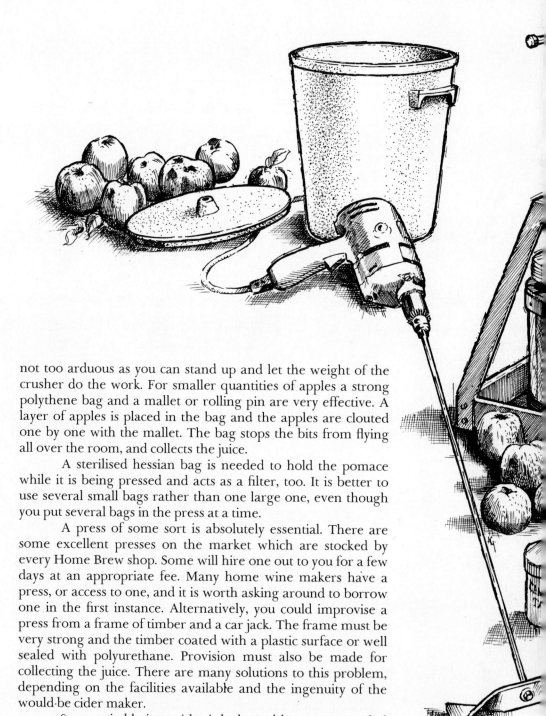

not too arduous as you can stand up and let the weight of the crusher do the work. For smaller quantities of apples a strong polythene bag and a mallet or rolling pin are very effective. A layer of apples is placed in the bag and the apples are clouted one by one with the mallet. The bag stops the bits from flying all over the room, and collects the juice.

A sterilised hessian bag is needed to hold the pomace while it is being pressed and acts as a filter, too. It is better to use several small bags rather than one large one, even though you put several bags in the press at a time.

A press of some sort is absolutely essential. There are some excellent presses on the market which are stocked by every Home Brew shop. Some will hire one out to you for a few days at an appropriate fee. Many home wine makers have a press, or access to one, and it is worth asking around to borrow one in the first instance. Alternatively, you could improvise a press from a frame of timber and a car jack. The frame must be very strong and the timber coated with a plastic surface or well sealed with polyurethane. Provision must also be made for collecting the juice. There are many solutions to this problem, depending on the facilities available and the ingenuity of the would-be cider maker.

Some suitable jars with air-locks and bungs are needed in which to ferment and mature the cider. A large polythene

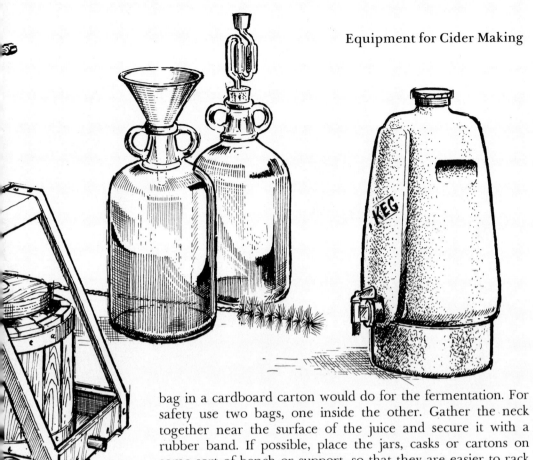

bag in a cardboard carton would do for the fermentation. For safety use two bags, one inside the other. Gather the neck together near the surface of the juice and secure it with a rubber band. If possible, place the jars, casks or cartons on some sort of bench or support, so that they are easier to rack without being moved. Five-gallon containers can be heavy to lift up on to a bench when full of cider. Plastic casks used for beer are equally suitable for cider, and being fitted with a tap are easy to rack. Polythene bins used for mashing beer are also suitable for cider. In fact, the home wine maker or brewer will have all the equipment needed, except perhaps the crusher and press, since the equipment is interchangeable. This includes an hydrometer and a trial jar, funnels, stirring spoons or paddles, bottles suitable for beer, crown caps and a capping tool.

Cleanliness is imperative. All equipment must be cleaned and sterilised before use. Two Campden tablets dissolved in 1 pint of water, to which has been added a large pinch of citric acid, makes a very effective sterilising solution. All surfaces that come into contact with the juice or cider must be sterilised to prevent the spoilage of the cider by micro-organisms.

Cider Making at Home

Since cider apples will not be available to most people, it is important to bear in mind the need to use a blend of sweet, bitter sweet, bitter sharp and sharp fruit. An approximate ratio for an average cider is three parts bitter and sweet to one part sharp. On this basis a fair quantity of dessert or eating apples are needed to provide the 'sweet' and some cooking apples to provide the 'sharp'. The 'bitter' can be obtained from some hard pears or from crab apples. The spherical, red Siberian or the egg-shaped, golden-red John Downie are suitable and fairly widely available from ornamental trees.

The precise quantities to use are not critical, for the measures that are appropriate in one autumn may not be appropriate in another after an indifferent season or with fruit grown in a different locality. These variations are sufficiently significant to make a mockery of precise calculations. It is enough simply to follow the general rule.

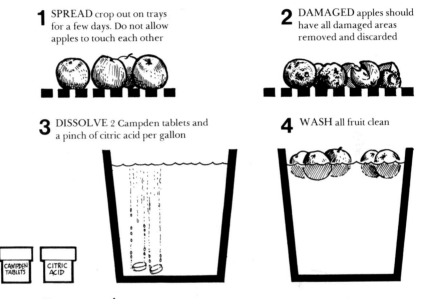

1 SPREAD crop out on trays for a few days. Do not allow apples to touch each other

2 DAMAGED apples should have all damaged areas removed and discarded

3 DISSOLVE 2 Campden tablets and a pinch of citric acid per gallon

4 WASH all fruit clean

CAMPDEN TABLETS

CITRIC ACID

Preparation

Leave the fruit on the tree as long as possible, and after it has been gathered, keep it spread out on trays for a few days to mellow. Fallen or damaged fruit may be used provided the bruised portions and/or maggot caves are first cut out and discarded. The apples should not be peeled or cored since the skin in particular contains colour as well as tannin and enzymes — all needed to make a good, clear cider.

Washing

All the fruit should be washed clean from leaves, twigs, grass, insects, dust and dirt. Use a deep sink or tub filled with cold water in which two Campden tablets and a pinch of citric acid per gallon (4.5 litres) have been dissolved. This will inhibit all microbes and so facilitate a better fermentation. It will also assist in the prevention of oxidation or browning of the fruit when it is crushed and exposed to the air. If it is not checked and the fruit becomes over-oxidised, an unpleasant taint develops in the finished cider.

79

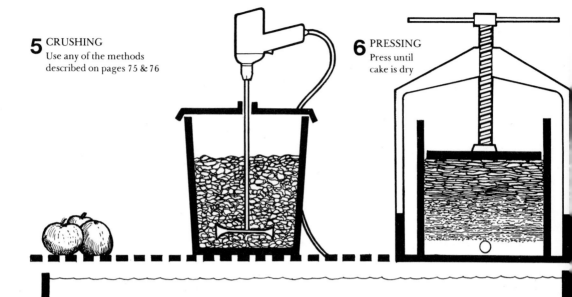

5 CRUSHING
Use any of the methods
described on pages 75 & 76

6 PRESSING
Press until
cake is dry

Crushing

As soon as the fruit is washed it should be crushed, taking care
not to crush the pips. If too many pips are damaged an
unpleasant bitterness is produced in the cider. Nevertheless, the
fruit should be thoroughly crushed into pulp and not just into
large pieces.

Pressing

Immediately a batch of fruit is crushed, it should be emptied
into a sterilised hessian bag in the press. The screw should be
turned and strong pressure applied to extract as much juice as
possible. As the juice runs from the press it should be collected
into a bin or jar containing **two crushed Campden tablets per
gallon of juice**. This will completely prevent oxidation and
effectively sterilise the juice.

When the flow of juice slows down almost to stopping,
release the pressure, open the bag and stir up the pulp. When
the pressure is reapplied a further flow of juice will be obtained.
This process should be repeated until the apple 'cake' is quite
dry.

Without a mechanical press it will not be possible to
obtain as high an extraction rate as is achieved commercially,
and 22lb (10kg) of apples may be needed to produce 9 pints (5
litres) of juice.

7 ADD CIDER APPLE CONCENTRATE
1 kg of concentrate to 35 pints
(20 litres) of apple juice +
2 Campden tablets

8 CHECK GRAVITY and if required adjust amount of
sugar to obtain a reading between 1.040 and 1.048

Improving the Juice

Since it is most unlikely that home-pressed apple juice will contain any cider apple juice, it is well worth adding some French cider apple concentrate. This is obtainable from many Home Brew shops in 1kg and 2.5kg cans. Just how much to use depends upon the quality and blend of the fruit you have and the kind of cider that you wish to make. For an average cider, 1kg of concentrate added to 35 pints (20 litres) of other apple juice is adequate, but more or less may be used as desired. But do add some to obtain genuine cider quality.

Checking for Sugar

A trial jar should now be filled with the blended juice and the gravity checked with an hydrometer. This simple and inexpensive instrument instantly measures the specific gravity of the juice and, by reference to the tables in Appendix A, the quantity of sugar in the juice and the amount of alcohol that this can produce. If need be, a little more sugar can be dissolved in the juice to increase the alcohol potential to the amount required.

An average cider should have a reading between 1.040 and 1.048. Stronger ciders take longer to mature and it is unwise to add more than sufficient sugar to obtain a reading between these two figures. Ordinary, white granulated household sugar should be used for preference since other sugars may alter the flavour. Honey would turn the cider into a mead called cyser.

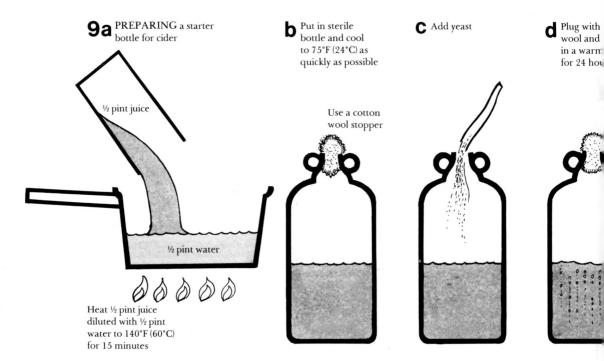

9a PREPARING a starter bottle for cider

½ pint juice

½ pint water

Heat ½ pint juice diluted with ½ pint water to 140°F (60°C) for 15 minutes

b Put in sterile bottle and cool to 75°F (24°C) as quickly as possible

Use a cotton wool stopper

c Add yeast

d Plug with wool and in a warm for 24 hou

Prepare the Yeast

Before the yeast is added it should be activated in some diluted fruit juice or malt extract. Heat ½ pint (0.25 litre) of juice and a ½ pint (0.25 litre) of water in a saucepan to 140°F (60°C) for fifteen minutes. Pour it into a sterilised bottle able to hold at least as much again. Plug the neck with cotton wool and cool the solution as quickly as possible to 75°F (24°C). Add the yeast and shake it well. Leave it in a warm place and within 24 hours the juice should be fermenting vigorously. This is enough to start the fermentation of a 1 gallon (5 litres) batch.

If a larger quantity of juice is to be fermented, sterilise ½ litre of juice and ½ litre of water as before. When it is cool, add half a teaspoonful of ammonium phosphate and one 3mg tablet of Vitamin B. Next, add the already well-fermenting ½ litre of diluted juice, plug the neck of the jar with cotton wool and leave in a warm place until the solution is fermenting vigorously. This is enough to start 6½ gallons (30 litres) of juice.

If an even larger quantity of juice is to be fermented, then repeat this process with 2 pints (1 litre) of juice and 2 pints (1 litre) of water, one teaspoonful of ammonium phosphate and two 3mg tablets of Vitamin B. These ingredients act as yeast nutrient and energiser and ensure a strong and healthy yeast colony. Add the fermenting yeast and, when this third batch is fermenting well, it is sufficient to start 15½ gallons (70 litres) of juice. The process can be repeated as necessary to start any quantity of juice. Always add approximately 5 per cent of the total juice in the form of an active yeast starter.

ADD ACTIVATED YEAST
to bulk of juice and
fit an air lock.
Leave to ferment at
59°F (15°C)

Fermentation

When the activated yeast has been stirred into the bulk of the juice, the vessel should be sealed with an air-lock and left in a cool place to ferment: 59°F (15°C) is about right. Fermentation will be relatively slow and all the better for that. If the fermentation is conducted at too high a temperature, some of the volatile esters that contribute to the bouquet and flavour will be driven off with the carbon dioxide. A steady even temperature encourages an equally even fermentation, free of stops and starts.

Stuck Ferment

Should the fermentation stop or become stuck prior to its conclusion, it may be necessary to prepare a fresh yeast starter. But first, thoroughly rouse the cider by giving it a good stir. This expels the carbon dioxide that could be inhibiting the fermentation and admits oxygen from the air which will encourage any living cells to reproduce themselves. Some yeast energiser in the form of ammonium phosphate and Vitamin B could also be stirred in to revitalise the yeast. Provided the temperature of the cider has not fallen below 41°F (5°C) nor risen above 95°F (35°C), fermentation should be resumed. If there has been a substantial temperature change, then clearly it must be adjusted to the norm of 59°F (15°C) as soon as possible.

Should fermentation not resume, make up a yeast starter and when this is fermenting well add an equal quantity of the stuck ferment. As soon as this is working add another equal quantity, and so on. Make sure that each new addition is fermenting well before the next addition. It is usually a waste of time to add the starter to the stuck ferment. Experience has shown that it is always more effective to add small quantities of the stuck ferment to the starter.

N.B. It is important to remember that sodium metabisulphite — Campden tablets — inhibit *all* micro-organisms, including yeast. It is essential, therefore, not to add the yeast to the sulphited juice until 24 hours later.

Racking

The term 'racking' is applied to the process of removing the clear or clearing cider from the sediment of fruit pulp particles and dead yeast cells that have fallen to the bottom of the container. The time to rack differs with the kind of cider being made.

To make a completely still and dry cider, the fermentation should be allowed to continue until the very end when the specific gravity has fallen to somewhere between 0.990 and 0.996.

To make a slightly lively cider, it should be racked into mineral water or beer bottles when the specific gravity has fallen to 1.002. Fermentation will continue slowly in the bottles and the resulting carbon dioxide will provide freshness and life to the mature cider.

It is unwise to rack at a higher specific gravity than 1.002 in case the cider stops fermenting altogether.

Racking is best accomplished by using a fermentation vessel fitted with a tap just above the floor of the vessel. All that needs to be done is to vent the cask, turn the tap and allow the cider to fall into a funnel leading to another container.

If the fermentation vessel does not have a tap, a siphon should be used. One end of a polythene tube is placed in the cider and sucked into the tube. When the tube is full, the end is pinched between finger and thumb and placed into a receiving vessel so situated that the top of the empty vessel is lower than the bottom of the full vessel. When the pressure between the finger and thumb is released, the force of gravity will draw the cider from the upper vessel into the lower vessel. By carefully tilting the upper container, all the clear cider can be drawn off, leaving only the sediment to be discarded.

The receiving vessel should be topped up with cider or with cold boiled water, sterilised glass marbles or pebbles until it is full. Now bung it tight with a softened bung, label it and put it into store for a few months.

Fining

If the cider is still hazy, the clearing process can be expedited by the admixture of finings. For small quantities some proprietary finings should be used. For larger quantities it would be more economical to use Bentonite Gel. This is available from Home Brew shops and instructions for its use are provided with it. More simple, and surprisingly effective with cider, is cow's milk. One tablespoonful per gallon is often enough, but if there is still a slight haze after a few days, repeat the dose. A heavy desposit will be formed from which the bright cider must be racked. It is important to keep the cider as cool as possible during the fining process and free from temperature changes that encourage thermal movement.

Filtering

Although filters suitable for home use can be bought, cider should not be filtered until an effort has been made to clear it by fining. Both fining and filtering, but especially filtering, should be looked upon as a last resort. Cider will usually clear naturally if left alone in a cool place free from vibration. Fining often removes some tannin from the cider and filtering at home inevitably exposes the cider to a great deal of air with its risk of oxidation and consequent flavour taint. If cider has to be filtered, one Campden tablet per gallon should be added to the receiving jar to diminish the oxidation.

Bottling

Cider benefits from six months' bulk maturation before bottling, but should not be left much longer. Beer bottles, cider bottles or mineral water bottles should be used. They should be washed thoroughly in clean hot water, rinsed with a sterilising solution as already described and drained dry. Each bottle should be filled to within 1in (3cm) of the top.

If a medium sweet cider is required, the non-fermentable sugar lactose may be stirred in at the rate of 4oz per gallon or 25g per litre. Alternatively, one or two saccharin tablets may be added to each bottle to suit your taste. If the cider is to be consumed immediately, it may be sweetened with caster sugar, but this cider should not subsequently be stoppered and stored in case a further fermentation is started. The pressure of the carbon dioxide might burst the bottle.

Once bottled, the cider should be left in a cool place until it is from four to eight months old. Younger than four months, the cider has not developed its full bouquet and flavour. Older than eight months, the cider might be just past its best, although still drinkable.

Blending

Few home cider makers may have the opportunity to make a number of different ciders in the course of a season. Those who are so blessed should try blending their ciders to improve them. One with too much tannin and astringency should be blended with one that is too bland and characterless — both will be improved. A cider that is too sharp could be blended for mutual benefit with another that has finished too sweet. All four could also be blended together to make an even better cider. A further suggestion is the blending of a thin and dull cider with some cider concentrate. Cider manufacturers practise blending on a huge scale. Home produced ciders would often be improved if they could be blended.

The one golden rule in blending is never to use an acetified, over-oxidised or bacterially infected cider with a sound cider. A bad cider will only ruin every other cider. Use only sound ciders, the flavour of which you wish to improve.

Sparkling Cider

The cider manufacturers merely impregnate their still ciders with carbon dioxide to produce a sparkling effect. Home cider makers may do the same with a soda siphon or sparkle their ciders naturally. At the bottling stage, rack a matured cider into a sterilised vessel and add to it a small amount of an activated champagne wine yeast and up to 1oz caster sugar per gallon (7g per litre). Stir well, fit an air-lock and leave the vessel in a warm place until the fermentation starts. Then bottle the cider into sterilised champagne wine bottles, leaving a head room of 1½in (4cm), and seal with a crown stopper very securely crimped. Lay the bottles on their sides for a couple of months, then stand them upright so that the sediment slides to the punt of the bottle.

Serve this cider quite cold and pour it carefully so as not to shake up or disturb the sediment. Well made and well fermented, this can be a superb drink. Since the cider will be very dry, it will be enjoyed the more if one or two saccharin tablets are put into each bottle before sealing. One merely takes the edge off the dryness, two gives a small measure of sweetness.

Vintage Cider

This is the cider of a single, exceptionally good gathering of apples. Unless home-produced ciders are blended, they will all be vintage ciders!

Cooking with Cider

The major cider manufacturers publish booklets and leaflets on this subject. They can be readily obtained from them free or for a few pence. Cider is particularly beneficial in the cooking of all bacon, ham and pork dishes, but can also be used very effectively with rabbit, poultry, fish and, of course, fresh fruit salads. Cider can be used in place of water or stock or boiled to reduce the quantity by half and, therefore, double the flavour. One of the advantages of making cider at home is that there is often a surplus that can be used for cooking. Ends of bottles or jars can be poured into a single bottle and, when this has cleared, the cider can be racked from the sediment and used for cooking.

Faults and Remedies

Over-oxidation. This is a flat, dull, 'brown' taste of the crushed apple, turned brown when exposed to the air. There is no effective remedy, but the fault can be prevented by sulphiting the apples and their juice as quickly as possible after crushing, and by the exclusion of air at all times.

Acetification. When damaged fruit is left lying about, it is visited by wasps, flies and other insects, any or all of which can carry bacteria of the mycoderma aceti family. As wild yeasts convert the fruit sugar into alcohol, the mycoderma aceti turn the weak alcohol into acetic acid. If this kind of fruit is included in the mash, then the acetic acid (vinegar) taint can spoil the cider flavour. Similarly, if the juice or cider is left open to the air and unprotected, the bacteria can cause an infection. Also, if pickles, chutneys or dishes involving vinegar are prepared at the same time as cider, the cider may well pick up the taint of vinegar.

There is no known remedy, but prevention is simple. Use only sound fruit, free from damaged portions. Sulphite adequately to inhibit the growth of micro-organisms such as mycoderma aceti. Keep the juice and cider protected from air-borne infection. Always sterilise vessels and utensils in case there are any invisible spoilage organisms in them.

Malo-lactic ferment. The main acid in apples is malic acid. By using a quantity of sharp apples in the blend, the cider will have an adequate acidity and no additional acid is normally required. If too many sharp apples are included and the concentration of malic acid is high, it is frequently reduced naturally by bacteria of the lacto-bacillus family, especially if the juice has not been very highly sulphited. This conversion of some of the sharp-tasting malic acid into the milder flavoured lactic acid usually occurs after fermentation has finished. An otherwise still cider may show the telltale ring of bubbles around the neck of the bottle two or three months after racking or bottling. The cider will have a slight 'petillance' when poured. If the bottles had been corked, wrongly, a few of these may be blown out.

This process is regarded as a fault if an entirely still cider is required. It can be prevented by adding one Campden tablet per gallon or per 5 litres at the time of the first racking. For most home-produced ciders using perhaps too many sharp apples, the process might be regarded as an advantage. The sharp-tasting cider mellows and is blessed with a fresh liveliness.

Yeastiness. When a yeast cell dies it begins to decay. If the dead yeast cells are not removed from the cider when fermentation finishes, the smell and taste of the decaying cells becomes impregnated in the cider. There is no remedy for this most unpleasant smell and taste but, again, it can easily be prevented. As soon as fermentation has finished, rack the clear or clearing cider from the sediment. As soon as another deposit appears, rack the cider again. If the dead yeast cells are taken out of the cider they cannot taint it, so take them out.

Ropiness. Sweet ciders are sometimes subject to attack by other members of the lacto-bacillus family, especially if they are low in acid and alcohol. The cider has a sheen, looks oily, and pours thickly. This is caused by long chains or ropes of bacteria. The remedy is to pour the cider into a bin and beat it with a wooden spoon to break up the ropes. Two crushed Campden tablets per gallon are then added and the cider is poured back into a jar and corked. Within a few days a deposit will have been thrown and the cider will look normal. Siphon it from the deposit into a clean jar or into bottles. The cider will have suffered no ill-effects and may safely be consumed.

It should be noted that this is a very rare occurrence, if the juice has been properly balanced and sulphited.

If you use good fruit, good yeast and good hygiene, you will have no faults in your cider and there will be no need to seek remedies, other than blending to improve the flavour.

Cider Recipes

Each recipe makes 4 gallons (18 litres) of cider. It is hardly worth the effort to make less and a single gallon is consumed so quickly as to be hardly noticed.

The specific varieties of apples where mentioned are not essential. What is important is that the apples used should be in roughly the same classification and proportion, i.e. sharp, bitter sweet and sweet, as those recommended.

Everyday Cider
9lb (4kg) cooking apples (sharp)
9lb (4kg) crab apples (bitter sweet)
18lb (8kg) eating apples (sweet)
4½lb (2kg) pears (bitter sweet)
1kg concentrated cider juice
12 pints (6.75 litres) water
9oz (250g) white sugar
Campden tablets
Champagne wine yeast

1. Wash, crush and press the fruit dry, add two crushed Campden tablets to the juice, cover it closely and leave it for 24 hours.
2. Dissolve the concentrated cider juice and sugar in some water and mix with the apple juice.
3. Add 1 quart of an activated champagne wine yeast.
4. Check the quantity and gravity of the cider must and adjust to 4 gallons (18 litres) at S.G. 1.046 by adding a little more water or sugar as necessary. (Different people with different fruit may extract more or less juice of a different gravity from others.)
5. Cover the vessel with a lid or sheet of polythene, so secured as not to prevent the escape of the carbon dioxide.
6. Leave the vessel in a coolish place until the fermentation finishes. This may take from three weeks to two months,

depending on the temperature and the quality of the fruit juice.

7. When fermentation finishes, give the cider a stir and then leave it to settle out, say, two or three days.

8. Rack the cider into a sterilised container and if it is still hazy, add some finings. As soon as the cider is clear, rack again and mature in bulk for four months.

9. Siphon the cider into sterilised bottles, seal them well and leave them for a month before serving.

Note. This is a basic, still, dry cider upon which variations can be made to suit your palate and your supply of fruit. The cider concentrate greatly improves the cider quality of your brew. The water is needed to dilute the concentrate. If the fruit is very juicy and a bit 'thin', some of the water can be omitted. The cider concentrate by itself will make up into 2 gallons (9 litres). The rest of the fruit should produce an equal quantity of juice, if it is well crushed and pressed. If you get more than 2 gallons of juice, then omit the quantity in excess of 2 gallons from the water. This will make a fuller-bodied cider.

The cider concentrate may be omitted and the water with it, but the resulting brew will be lacking in some of the cider flavour that the concentrate confers.

Not more than 1oz of priming sugar per gallon may be stirred in at the bottling stage to produce an effervescent, sparkling cider, full of freshness and vitality. Since the cider will be quite dry, you may also need to add from six to twelve crushed saccharin pellets per gallon with the priming sugar.

Country Cider

40lb (18kg) Yarlington Mill or Dabinette or any of the Jersey varieties mentioned on p. 71 (all bitter sweet)
20lb (9kg) John Downie or Siberian crab apples (bitter sweet)
20lb (9kg) Bramley or Lord Derby (both sharp)
Champagne wine yeast
Campden tablets

1. Wash, crush and press the apples, add 4 crushed Campden tablets, cover and leave for 24 hours.
2. Add an activated yeast and ferment to a finish.
3. Rack, bottle and mature as already described.

Sweet Cider

30lb (13.5kg) assorted cooking apples — Blenheim, Bramley,
    Derby, James Grieve, Granny Smith
40lb (18kg) assorted eating apples — Cox's Orange Pippin,
    Golden Delicious, Russet, Worcester Pearmain
10lb (4.5kg) John Downie and Siberian crab apples
1kg cider concentrate
1 level tsp grape tannin
Champagne wine yeast
Campden tablets

1. Wash, crush and press the fruit, add four crushed Campden
   tablets, cover and leave for 24 hours.
2. Stir in the cider concentrate, grape tannin and activated
   yeast.
3. Measure the quantity of must and its specific gravity.

   If you have more than 4 gallons with a specific gravity
   lower than 1.060, add some sugar to increase the gravity to that
   figure.

   If the quantity is less than 4 gallons but the gravity is
   1.060 or above, so be it. If the gravity is below 1.060, add some
   sugar until the figure is reached.
4. Fit a lid or air-lock and ferment as usual, but check the
   gravity from time to time and when it is down to 1.010, rack
   the cider from its sediment into a clean vessel.
5. Add 1g potassium sorbate and one Campden tablet per
   gallon to terminate fermentation. Move the vessel to a cold
   place and leave it for a few days for the sediment to settle.
6. As soon as the cider is clear, rack it again, add one Campden
   tablet per gallon, and mature it in bulk until it is six months
   old.

Scrumpy

Assorted apples and pears
Sugar as required
Campden tablets
Wine yeast

Mix as many eating apples as you can get with an equal
quantity of cooking apples, some firm pears, some crab apples
and even some quince. The small yellow fruit of the garden
Japanese quince will do very well.

All the fruit may be windfalls but clean it up first, removing the bruised portions and maggot caves. This is best done after washing the fruit clean. As the damaged portions are cut out, the good portions can be dropped into a bin containing two crushed Campden tablets and a half teaspoonful of citric acid dissolved in a gallon of water. This will keep the fruit white and free from oxidation until it is wanted for crushing and pressing.

When all the fruit has been cleaned, crushed and pressed, add one crushed Campden tablet per gallon and measure the specific gravity. If it is under 1.040, add sufficient sugar to raise the gravity to that figure. If it is above, then cover the vessel and leave it for 24 hours.

Next day, stir in an activated wine yeast, cover the vessel and leave the cider to ferment out. An occasional stir will help it.

When fermentation has finished and the cider begins to clear, rack it into sterilised jars to mature for some months.

Before bottling, taste the scrumpy and, if necessary, sweeten it to your taste with saccharin. Scrumpy tends to make better draught cider than bottled, but put it in containers of a size that you can empty within a few days. Alternatively, put it in a beer pressure keg and treat it as explained on p. 49 for draught beer. It is particularly effective in this way.

No precise quantities are given for scrumpy, since it is essentially a simple cider of the kind made on isolated farms. Each one is different. Use all your spare apples and those of your neighbours and friends. Make as much as you have facilities for crushing, pressing, fermenting and storing. Indeed, if you have to use an excess of cooking apples, then do so. Remove some of the excess acid by adding to the juice, when first pressed, ½oz of precipitated chalk per gallon (15g per 5 litres). This will reduce the acidity by about one-third. There will be much foaming and cloudiness, but this will clear in a day or so and the juice can then be siphoned off the pasty sediment. Do not forget to keep the juice protected with one crushed Campden tablet per gallon during this time.

After racking the juice, add an activated wine yeast and continue as already described.

Cider Vinegar

Having made a good quantity of cider, you will certainly want to make some cider vinegar. It is simplicity itself, but a word of warning must be given at the outset. Do be careful not to make vinegar at the same time as cider or beer or wine, nor in the same room, nor with equipment also used for another beverage. No matter how careful you are, there is a risk of contamination if you ignore this warning.

Use a cider that started with a specific gravity of around 1.046, that fermented out to dryness and has not been sweetened. Decide how much cider vinegar you wish to make and mix with it one portion of cider, wine or malt vinegar to five portions of cider. This could be two and a half pints of cider and half a pint of vinegar or one and a quarter litres of cider and a quarter litre of vinegar.

Plug the bottle with cotton wool

Pour the mixture into a container capable of holding twice the quantity or a little more, e.g. a gallon jar or polythene vessel. Plug the neck with cotton wool to keep out flies and air-borne microbes but to let in filtered air. Leave the vessel in a warm kitchen for a period of three months.

The cider will first go hazy, then a skin will form on the surface. Eventually, the cider vinegar will clear and will be ready for pasteurisation.

Carefully siphon the cider vinegar into a large stew pan, cover it, place it on a stove, bring the temperature up to 140°F (60°C) and hold it there for fifteen minutes. The cider vinegar should now be bottled in warmed, sterilised bottles, sealed and labelled. It is ready for use as soon as it is cool.

If a portion of vinegar is left in the container, five more portions of cider may be added to it and another batch started.

Cider vinegar keeps well, has a mild flavour and is an excellent ingredient to use in vinaigrette sauces and in marinading and cooking bacon joints, ham, pork and fish. Indeed, it can be used successfully in place of any other vinegar.